P9-AQS-720

ANDY WARHOL
Fighting to Revolutionize Art

ANDY WARHOL

Fighting to Revolutionize Art

E

Enslow Publishing
101 W. 23rd Street
Suite 240
New York, NY 10011
USA

enslow.com

Edward Willett

Published in 2018 by Enslow Publishing, LLC.
101 W. 23rd Street, Suite 240, New York, NY 10011

Library of Congress Cataloging-in-Publication Data

Names: Willett, Edward, 1959- author.
Title: Andy Warhol : fighting to revolutionize art / by Edward Willett.
Description: New York : Enslow Publishing, 2018. | Series: Rebels with a cause | Includes bibliographical references and index. | Audience: Grades 7-12.
Identifiers: LCCN 2017031811 | ISBN 9780766092594 (library bound) | ISBN 9780766095489 (paperback)
Subjects: LCSH: Warhol, Andy, 1928-1987—Juvenile literature. | Artists—United States—Biography—Juvenile literature.
Classification: LCC N6537.W28 W575 2017 | DDC 700.92 [B] —dc23
LC record available at https://lccn.loc.gov/201703181

Printed in China

To Our Readers: We have done our best to make sure all website addresses in this book were active and appropriate when we went to press. However, the author and the publisher have no control over and assume no liability for the material available on those websites or on any websites they may link to. Any comments or suggestions can be sent by email to customerservice@enslow.com.

Portions of this book originally appeared in the book *Andy Warhol "Everyone Will be Famous for 15 Minutes"*.

Photo Credits: Cover, p. 1 Nancy R. Schiff/Archive Photos/Getty Images; p. 7 Nicolas Asfouri/AFP/Getty Images; p. 10 Catherine McGann/Archive Photos/Getty Images; p. 13 Michael Ochs Archives/Getty Images; pp. 19, 82, 98 Bettmann/Getty Images; pp. 21, 38, 49, 68 Herve Gloaguen/Gamma-Rapho/Getty Images; p. 24 Apic/Hulton Archive/Getty Images; p. 26 Robert R. McElroy/Archive Photos/Getty Images; pp. 32, 34, 86 Jack Mitchell/Archive Photos/Getty Images; p. 40 Robert Alexander/Archive Photos/Getty Images; pp. 42, 110 Archie Carpenter/Getty Images; pp. 44–45, 52 Mario De Biasi/Mondadori Portfolio/Getty Images; p. 55 Santi Visalli/Archive Photos/Getty Images; p. 59 Vernon Shibla/New York Post Archives/Getty Images; p. 61 John Springer Collection/Corbis Historical/Getty Images; p. 64 Everett Collection Inc./Alamy Stock Photo; p. 72 New York Daily News Archive/Getty Images; p. 79 Jack Smith/New York Daily News Archive/Getty Images; p. 84 © AP Images; p. 88 Ken Heyman/Woodfin Camp/The LIFE Images Collection/Getty Images; pp. 90–91, 96 Robin Platzer/The LIFE Images Collection/Getty Images; p. 103 Patrick McMullan/Getty Images; p. 105 Jeffrey M. Frank/Shutterstock.com; p. 109 RDA/Hulton Archive/Getty Images; p. 111 Vanessa Carvalho/LatinContent/Getty Images; interior pages graphic element Eky Studio/Shutterstock.com.

CONTENTS

INTRODUCTION

N obody had ever seen anything quite like the art exhibition that opened July 9, 1962, in the Ferus Gallery in Los Angeles. Thirty-two paintings of Campbell's Soup cans (one for each flavor) were displayed on a shelf as if they were real cans. Each measured twenty by twenty-six inches, and each was priced at $100.

Only six sold (one to actor Dennis Hopper). Another gallery not far away bought a bunch of real soup cans, put them in the windows, and offered three for just sixty cents.[1]

But while the soup paintings didn't attract buyers, they attracted publicity. Two months before, on May 11, 1962, *TIME* magazine had said that "a segment of the advance guard" of painters had decided that "the most banal and even vulgar trappings of modern civilization can, when transposed literally to canvas, become Art."

A thirty-year-old New York–based commercial artist named Andy Warhol, then engaged in painting soup cans, of all things, was quoted as saying, "I just paint things I

While considered strange and unique—and unsellable—when he first produced them, Warhol's soup can images have since gone on to be some of the most famous and recognizable works of art.

always thought were beautiful, things you use every day and never think about. I just do it because I like it."[2]

TIME called the new style "the Slice-of-Cake School," but the name it finally ended up with was Pop Art. Before long, Warhol would become the Prince of Pop and its most famous creator. That fame outlasted the Pop Art movement. Warhol once famously said, "In the future everybody will be world-famous for fifteen minutes."[3] While alive, he spent more than a quarter century as a world-renowned art star, and now, more than thirty years after his death, he's still as famous and controversial as ever.

Back in 1962, gallery owner Irving Blum bought all the *Campbell's Soup Can* paintings back from the handful of purchasers and bought the rest of the set from Warhol for $1,000. In 1996, the Museum of Modern Art (MoMa) acquired them from Blum for an estimated $15 million.[4]

Warhol, a true American rebel and a trendsetter rather than a trend follower, would have loved that.

1

A Colorful Childhood

ndy Warhol was born Andrew Warhola in Pittsburgh, Pennsylvania, on August 6, 1928, the youngest son of Ondrej and Julia Warhola. His parents were both from the Ruthenian village of Miková, Slovakia, located in the Carpathian Mountains near the borders of Russia and Poland.

After the end of the First World War, Ondrej started trying to bring Julia to the US, where he had moved years earlier. He sent her the fare five times in 1919, but none of the money reached her. In 1921, she borrowed $180 from a priest and finally made it to Pittsburgh. In 1922, the couple's first son, Paul, was born; their second, John, was born in 1925.

By the time Andy was born in 1928, Ondrej was often away for work for weeks or months; he was employed by a company that built roads and moved houses to make way for new construction. Julia still couldn't speak English.

The Depression Hits Home

As the Great Depression took hold, Ondrej lost his job. Fortunately, he had several thousand dollars in savings, which allowed him to feed his family, but forced them to

Andy Warhol's childhood home in Pittsburgh, Pennsylvania. Andy first discovered his love of art—and celebrity—while living in this house with his family.

move into a two-room apartment where Paul, John, and Andy had to sleep in the same bed. In the overcrowded conditions, Paul and John often fought each other. Julia began working part-time, cleaning houses and making sculptures out of tin cans. Paul sold newspapers on streetcars.

When Andy was four years old, his father regained his job and was once again called away frequently, leaving Paul, age ten, as head of the household. Paul, who hadn't been able to speak English when he started school and had also developed a speech impediment, began to skip school and to take out some of his frustrations by disciplining his little brother. Paul later said that Andy

10

was picking up bad language from kids in the street. "The more you smacked him, the more he said it, the worse he got."[1]

In September of 1932, Paul decided that four-year-old Andy should be registered for school. But he was two years younger than any of the other students, and on the first day a girl slapped him. Hearing this, Julia decided that Andy shouldn't be forced to go back. For the next two years, while Paul and John were in school, Andy was alone with his mother.

THE GREAT DEPRESSION

Between 1929 and 1939, the United States fell into the worst economic downturn in history. After stock prices fell in 1929, the rest of the economy followed. Prices for agricultural goods fell by as much as sixty percent, and unemployment rose to twenty-five percent in the United States. Millions of people across the country, both rich and poor, lost everything they had, including their savings, jobs, and homes. Families like the Warholas were forced to send even their children to work in order to simply scrape by. The United States didn't fully recover from the Great Depression until World War II. Many economists believe that war spending finally brought the country out of the hole it was in and helped the nation recover.

Besides making flower sculptures, Julia drew pictures (her favorite subjects were angels and cats), embroidered, and loved decorating Easter eggs.[2] When she was alone with Andy, she would draw pictures with him: portraits of each other, sometimes, or pictures of the cat.

New Neighborhood, New Friends

In early 1934, the Warhola family moved again, into a two-story brick house in Pittsburgh's Oakland neighborhood, their nicest house yet. Andy and John shared a bedroom; Paul had his own bedroom in the attic. There were lots of boys around to play with, but a neighbor remembered that, "Andy was so intelligent, he was more or less in a world all of his own, he kept to himself like a loner."[3]

When Andy did play with other children, he usually preferred to play with girls. His first best friend at Holmes Elementary School, located just half a block from the new house, was a little Ukrainian girl named Margie Girman. On Saturday mornings, they went to the movie theater, where, for just eleven cents, children got an ice-cream bar, a double feature, and a signed eight-by-ten glossy photograph of one of the stars, which Andy collected; he soon had a whole box of them.

Andy liked school now, and did well in it—and all the time he was drawing. Julia encouraged him, even buying a movie projector so he could watch black-and-white silent cartoons.

Sick and Tired

As a child, Andy had several health problems. When he was two, his eyes would swell up and had to be washed

After college, Warhol moved to New York City to become an artist, but he stayed close with his family, and especially his mother, Julia, who would later move in with him in New York.

with boric acid every day. When he was four, he broke his arm after tripping over the streetcar tracks. Nobody realized it was broken until it had healed crookedly; the doctors had to re-break it so it could heal straight. When he was six, he had scarlet fever. When he was seven, he had his tonsils removed.

And then, in the autumn of 1936, when he was eight years old, he came down with rheumatic fever.

> **"I learned when I was little that whenever I got aggressive and tried to tell someone what to do nothing happened—I just couldn't carry it off. I learned that you actually have more power when you shut up, because at least some people will start to maybe doubt themselves."[4]**

A complication of strep throat, rheumatic fever produces inflammation in the body that can damage the heart, joints, skin, and brain.[5] If the brain is affected, the inflammation can cause loss of coordination and uncontrolled movement of the limbs and face, commonly called St. Vitus's dance.

Andy found that when he tried to draw on the blackboard his hand would begin to shake. He had trouble writing his name or tying his shoes. The other kids laughed at him and began to pick on him. Suddenly, school became terrifying. The family doctor ordered Andy stay in bed for a month.

Andy loved it. He had his mother all to himself and didn't have to deal with bullies. His mother gave him movie magazines, comic books, and coloring books and moved the radio into the dining room, where his bed had been placed. Once his hands stopped shaking, Andy spent hours coloring, making collages with cut-up magazines, and playing with paper dolls.

After four weeks, he suffered a relapse and had to go back to bed for another four weeks. After the second month, he developed another complication: large reddish-brown patches on his skin. Rheumatic fever can also cause lumps or nodules to appear beneath normal-looking skin, and bad skin would plague Andy for the rest of his life.

While he would be saddled with complications for years to come, those eight weeks in bed were important to

LIKE MOTHER, LIKE SON

While Andy Warhol was home in bed with rheumatic fever, he was encouraged by his mother to indulge in his love of art, a passion that the two shared. Although she was a mother and housewife during Andy's childhood and only occasionally got to indulge in her own artistic passion, when Andy grew up, she eventually followed in her son's footsteps. After moving to New York City to live with Andy, Julia began helping him at work, lending her talents to hand lettering to her son's advertising campaigns. She also illustrated a few books in the 1950s. Julia was eventually recognized for her work in 1958, when the American Institute of Graphic Arts presented her with an award for her lettering on an album cover she'd worked on.

Andy Warhol's eventual development as an artist. In the magazines and through the radio, he immersed himself in a rich fantasy world, one filled with celebrities and centered on Hollywood and New York. His fascination with celebrities would be a driving force for much of his career.

2
Welcome to New York

At the end of the 1930s, Ondrej was still working twelve hours a day, six days a week. Then, while working in Wheeling, West Virginia, he and several other men accidentally drank contaminated water. When he came home, he became so ill that he was confined to bed.

Andy was fourteen when Ondrej went into the hospital for a series of tests. He never came out, dying five days later. The body was laid out in the house for three days, with someone keeping vigil by it every night. Andy refused to look at it and instead hid under his bed.[1] For the rest of his life he had such a fear of death that his father's funeral was probably the last one he attended until his own.

Then Julia fell ill. Her doctor diagnosed her with colon cancer. Her only chance of survival was to undergo a colostomy, a still-experimental operation in which her entire bowel system was cut out and replaced with a bag on her stomach.

The operation was successful, and Julia recovered remarkably well, but the experience was traumatic for Andy. Now, along with his fear of funerals, he developed a horror of hospitals and surgeons that would remain with him his whole life—and may have contributed to his death.

An Artist's Education

Through all of this upheaval, Andy had his art, and Pittsburgh was a great place to study it. The public schools specialized in teaching it, and the city was home to three art-loving, wealthy families—the Carnegies, the Mellons, and the Fricks—who sponsored art competitions, art centers, and, most importantly to Andy, free Saturday-morning art classes for talented children at the Carnegie Museum.

In 1937, at age nine, Andy was recommended for the Carnegie Museum course by Annie Vickermann, his art teacher at Holmes Elementary School. Students had to be recommended by their teachers, but the art supplies were free.

Andy's teacher, James Fitzpatrick, immediately saw something unique in Andy. "He was so individualistic and ahead of his time. He was magnificently talented."

But, he added, Andy was also "a little bit obnoxious. He had no consideration for other people . . . He was socially inept . . . He was not pleasant."[2]

Meanwhile, in September 1941, Andy began attending Schenley High School, a twenty-minute walk from his house. Andy drew almost constantly, his artwork piling up around the house to the point that his mother once dumped a bunch of drawings in the trash. "He wasn't in the art club because his talent was so superior to the rest of us," remembered Lee Karageorge, a classmate of Andy's.[3]

Warhol's love of art began in high school, when he not only grew as an artist, but found his love of the movies and popular culture. Little did he know he'd go on to become a part of that culture himself one day.

Aside from his art classes, the greatest influence on Andy during high school was probably the movies. He also read lots of magazines and newspapers, and would cut out photographs to use in collages and drawings.

Andy was focused on getting accepted to college, and in his senior year, he won acceptances from both the University of Pittsburgh and the Carnegie Institute of Technology. He decided to attend Carnegie Tech.

College Knowledge

At university, Andy soon ran into trouble. His strong Eastern European accent made him hard to understand. Nor could he write grammatically, relying on two classmates, Ellie Simon and Gretchen Schmertz, to help him write his papers.

But even in art classes he had difficulties. He kept coming up with things he hadn't been assigned to do, and his work wasn't what the instructors were used to. Several times his freshman year he was on the verge of being dropped from the university for failing to maintain the necessary standards.

It helped that Andy managed to elicit sympathy from the department secretary, Lorene Twiggs. He would tell her how difficult things were at home and always dressed in worn-out clothes. When, at the end of his freshman year, the art department decided to drop many of its freshman students (including Andy) to make room for veterans returning from the just-ended Second World War, Andy burst into tears, and Mrs. Twiggs put up a fight for him. In the end, the faculty decided to put him on probation: he had to produce new work over the summer and reapply for admission in the fall.

Over the summer he took a sketchbook with him while he helped his brother Paul sell fruits and vegetables door-to-door. His lightning-fast sketches of the people they saw in the streets earned him readmission to the art department—and won him a $40 prize, the first cash he'd ever earned with his art, for the best summer work done by a sophomore.

The prize drew new attention to Andy, and he fell in with a group of (in biographer Victor Bockris's words)

According to his high school art teacher, Warhol, shown here working on an art project at the Factory in 1966, was always a few steps ahead of the times.

"striking, stimulating . . . noisy, outspoken, argumentative, high-spirited"[4] friends who helped protect and nurture the child-like Andy through his remaining years of university.

Andy joined the student film club. He attended symphony concerts. He became interested in ballet and took a modern dance class. He also went to parties, which would be another life-long love of his. "He glowed,"

THE BAUHAUS

Das Staatliches Bauhaus, created in Germany at the end of the First World War by Walter Gropius, was an institute for experimenting with architecture, industrial art, and handicraft. At its heart was an ideology that said art and technology should be integrated, to the benefit of both; that the previously separate roles of artist and craftsman should be united, and the resulting aesthetic applied to everything from architecture to household appliances to typefaces.[6] The Bauhaus made art a business—as would Andy Warhol.

remembered Leonard Kessler, one of his college friends. "You could see the little cherubic face lighting up."[5]

Andy's instructors in the Painting and Design faculty taught him that fine art and commercial art were one and the same; that the distinction between them was entirely artificial. It was a philosophy heavily influenced by the Bauhaus, and it, in turn, heavily influenced Warhol in the years to come.

The Blotted Line

Sometime while he was at Carnegie Tech, Andy developed the drawing technique that would later make his commercial art unique. He would first copy a line drawing onto a piece of non-absorbent paper, then hinge that paper with tape to a second sheet of more absorbent paper. He'd ink over a small section of the lines on the first sheet with an old fountain pen, then fold over the second piece of paper and lightly press it to the first to absorb or "blot" the ink. Large drawings had to be done in sections, which made it a very time-consuming process. The resulting image was unique, with dotted, broken and delicate lines. The blotted image could then be colored in various ways.[7]

Sometimes Andy would use images from magazines in these drawings, tracing a chair from a photograph, then using the blotted-line technique to transfer his tracing to a new piece of paper.

From the beginning, his art was controversial. A painting showing a woman nursing a dog instead of a baby was removed from a department exhibition. In March 1949, a painting of a little boy with his finger up his nose that Andy submitted to the annual Pittsburgh Associated Artists exhibition was rejected after half the jurors thought it was an insult. (The other half thought it was an important work.) The scandal drew even more attention to Andy's work.

Andy also began experimenting with changing his name at Carnegie Tech. As art director of the university literary magazine, *The Cano*, he called himself Andrew Warhola. On his self-designed Christmas card, he signed his name as André. He sometimes signed paintings Andrew Warhol, but to his friends he was, as he would eventually be for everyone, Andy.

In 1948, Andy, then nineteen, got his first commercial art job, painting backdrops for a prominent Pittsburgh

STAATLICHES BAUHAUS
AUSSTELLUNG
JULI SEPT
WEIMAR
1923

The Bauhaus style, displayed here, was a big influence on Warhol's own work. Thanks to Warhol, Pop Art would be just as big a movement as Bauhaus.

department store. He used some of the money to travel to New York with Philip Pearlstein and Art Elias to look at modern art—and look for job opportunities.

Tina S. Fredericks, art director of *Glamour*, liked his portfolio and promised him work as soon as he graduated. After he graduated, though, Andy wasn't entirely certain he wanted to go to New York. According to his brother John, he sent his portfolio to a school in Indiana, and only when they rejected him did he finally decide to go to New York.[8]

New York, New York

Just one week after graduation, in June 1949, Warhol and his friend Philip Pearlstein moved into a shabby apartment on New York's Lower East Side. Both men would go on to be leading figures in major art movements, Pearlstein in Contemporary Realism and Warhol in Pop.

At the time, almost no one could make a living as a fine artist. The real money was in commercial art, as the post-war economy boomed and advertising became big business.

True to her word, Tina S. Fredericks hired Andy to draw shoes for *Glamour*, launching a successful commercial career and making him a New York fixture. Near the end of the summer of 1949, not long after Andy turned twenty-one, *Glamour* published his first drawing, of girls climbing a ladder. The credit listed his name as Andy Warhol.

Art directors of the time liked the way Andy's commercial art seemed to show he was having fun, not somehow lowering himself to draw pictures of shoes and clothes and furniture. "The impression he left was of this

Warhol's love of art didn't always remain on the canvas. Although he got his start working with paintings and drawings, he'd later go on to explore other mediums — including sculpture and film.

IF THE SHOE FITS

After moving to New York City, the first order of business was for Andy to find a job, and he lucked out, landing a freelance job with *Glamour* magazine, one of the best-selling women's magazines. He was commissioned to draw shoes for the fashion-forward magazine, and his drawings and paintings were so well received that he soon was taking calls from other publications looking to include his work in their pages. *Esquire* magazine, a leading men's lifestyle publication, was his next major client. They hired Andy to illustrate their accessories column, where he sketched all sorts of men's fashion items—including, of course, shoes.

eager, interested person, who drew beautifully," recalled George Klauber.[9]

Work poured in. Andy drew for *Glamour*, for *Charm*, for *Seventeen*. He did album covers for Columbia Records. But he still felt like an outsider, on the fringes of the beautiful celebrity world he aspired to.

Warhol's work continued to draw attention. He worked on book jackets and even appeared on television: NBC would show his hand on the morning news program, drawing the weather map.

A piece he'd drawn of a sailor injecting heroin, to promote a radio documentary, was published as a full-page ad in the *New York Times* on September 13, 1951, earning him more money than anything else he'd ever done. It was used on the cover of the recording of the program, and, in 1953, won Warhol the Art Director's Club gold medal, the top award in the advertising art industry.

A Secret Life

Warhol was gay, and in the 1950s, homosexuality was both against the law and completely unacceptable in mainstream society. He found his way into the underground LGBTQ community, but he was more interested in its glamour than in sex. (Warhol once said the most interesting thing about sex was not doing it.) He tended to form crushes on beautiful but unobtainable young men, and often complained about his "boy problems."[10] When he did form close relationships with men, they inevitably fell apart after a few months.

On June 16, 1952, Warhol put on his first solo show. The show featured illustrations based on the stories in Truman Capote's book *Other Voices, Other Rooms*. It opened at the Hugo Gallery—his first tentative step into the world of fine art.

The show flopped. The director of the Hugo Gallery, Alexander Iolas, had put up the show very late in the season because he was so impressed with Warhol's work. Unfortunately, it was so late that almost everyone important in New York's art community was in Europe when it opened.

15 Drawings Based on the Writings of Truman Capote featured delicate drawings of boys, butterflies, and cupids, splashed with magenta and violet. "The work has an air of precocity, of carefully studied perversity," wrote James

Fitzsimmons in *Art Digest*.[11] But very few people saw it, although Truman Capote and his mother, Nina, showed up before the show closed, much to Warhol's delight.

None of the pieces, priced at around $300, sold. However, Andy had made a very important contact in David Mann, the gallery manager, who went on to work for the Bodley Gallery. This gallery mounted three Warhol shows between 1956 and 1959.

In the spring of 1953, Warhol obtained an agent, Fritzie Miller, and with her help landed assignments with giant magazines like *McCall's*, *Ladies' Home Journal*, *Vogue*, and *Harper's Bazaar*. "Whatever he illustrated—shampoo or bras or jewelry or lipstick or perfume—there was a decorative originality about his work that made it eye catching," *New Yorker* art critic Calvin Tomkins wrote in 1970.[12]

Warhol, just twenty-five years old, was becoming the most sought-after illustrator of women's accessories in New York—and beginning to make quite a lot of money doing it, although he tended to waste it on extravagances like breakfast at the Plaza Hotel. He did, however, invest in a better place to live, and he moved in with his mother and a large (and variable) number of cats.

That same year, Warhol began a brief affair with Alfred Carlton (Carl) Willers. They met in the photo collection of the New York Public Library, and Willers became a frequent visitor to Warhol's apartment, although Julia thought he was just another of Andy's friends. Carl and Andy remained friends for many years, though their physical relationship was short-lived. Warhol later said that he was twenty-five when he had his first sexual experience, and twenty-six when he stopped.

"Everything Was Wonderful"

Warhol continued to try to break into the world of fine art. In 1954, he had three shows at the Loft Gallery. He was part of a group show in April, followed by a solo exhibition consisting of marbled paper sculptures with small figures drawn on them, and then a show made up of drawings of a dancer, John Butler. Art directors from major advertising agencies attended the opening, but the show was almost ignored in the fine-art world.

At the Loft Gallery, Warhol met Vito Giallo, assistant to the well-known graphic artist Jack Wolfgang, in whose studio the gallery operated. Shortly afterward, Warhol hired Giallo as his first assistant. Warhol "was always positive about everything in life," Giallo recalled. "Everything was wonderful."[13]

That fall, Warhol fell in love with Charles Lisanby, a set designer for television and Broadway. "He was interested in the fact that I was working in television and because other very fine artists like Ben Shahn worked in television occasionally," Lisanby said. "Andy wanted to do that. Andy always wanted to do anything that was going to get him publicity . . . The one thing then that he wanted more than anything else was to be famous."[14] The relationship cooled after a disastrous trip around the world together in 1956.

In 1955, Warhol got his biggest commercial account yet: a weekly ad in the Sunday *New York Times* for I. Miller, a Manhattan shoe store. The ads were a huge success. That fall, Warhol replaced Vito Giallo with Nathan Gluck, his assistant for the next nine years. He also had his first show at the Bodley Gallery, where David Mann had gone after leaving the Hugo Gallery. Reviewers were not impressed and only a couple of drawings sold, at very low prices. Nevertheless, Mann was able to get some of the drawings included in the Recent Drawings show at the Museum of Modern Art.

In December 1956, Warhol's *Crazy Golden Slippers* show at the Bodley Gallery opened, featuring large blotted-line paintings of shoes painted gold, or decorated with gold metal and foil. Each was given the name of a celebrity: Judy Garland, James Dean, Julie Andrews, etc. The show was featured in a two-page color spread in *Life Magazine* . . . but *Life* described him as a commercial artist who had created the pieces as a hobby.[15]

Today, the *Crazy Golden Slippers* show is seen as the first real attempt to bridge "high" and "low" culture that was central to Warhol's work throughout his career. In February 2015, "Golden Shoe (Julie Andrews Shoe)," originally purchased by Charles Lisanby, was sold at auction in London for £722,500 (around $857,000), a world auction record for any Warhol piece from the 1950s.

Amanda Lo Iacono, writing for the auction house, Christie's, notes that the work was "a comment on Warhol's interest in the connection between commodification and celebrity, themes that would go on to define his practice."[16]

By 1957, Warhol was so successful financially that he established Andy Warhol Enterprises on the advice of his accountant. But he was still seen as just a commercial artist, not a serious one.

An Earthquake in the Art World

But in the "serious" art world, the rules were changing, as two new artists, Jasper Johns and Robert Rauschenberg, led a move away from Abstract Expressionism.

Artist Jasper Johns was a commercial artist like Warhol, but unlike Warhol, Johns was immediately taken seriously in the fine art world, selling pieces to such buyers as the Museum of Modern Art.

Like Warhol, Rauschenberg, also a commercial artist, embraced popular culture. He started using unusual materials and methods, painting with house paint or putting ink on the wheel of a car and then running it over paper. His first solo exhibition at the Leo Castelli Gallery in 1959 featured works that he called combines: three-dimensional collages. *Monogram*, for instance, combined a stuffed angora goat, a tire, a police barrier, the heel of a shoe, a tennis ball, and paint.[17]

Jasper Johns, who had created Tiffany's window displays with Rauschenberg, painted targets, maps, and flags. Leo Castelli discovered Johns's work while visiting Rauschenberg's studio, and was so impressed he offered him a show on the spot—a year before Rauschenberg's own show.[18]

Flags, Targets, and Numbers sold out. The Museum of Modern Art bought four pieces. Instead of the intense personal vision of the Abstract Expressionists, Johns painted commonplace objects in such a way that, as he put it, "There may or may not be an idea, and the meaning may just be that the painting exists."[19]

Rauschenberg and Johns were both commercial artists who had worked for some of the same people Warhol had. Unlike Warhol, they'd been immediately taken seriously. But if they could do it, Warhol figured, so could he. He began going regularly to the Leo Castelli Gallery, hoping to break in.

At about the same time, Warhol met Emile de Antonio, an artist's agent who would become famous later as a documentary director. Tina S. Fredericks, who introduced the men, described de Antonio as "a catalyst who could, almost miraculously, put his finger on what direction talent ought to take." According to Fredericks, Andy credited de Antonio with being the first person he met who saw "commercial art as real art and real art as commercial art, and he made the whole New York art world see it that way, too."[20]

But Warhol's last show of the 1950s, *Wild Raspberries*—watercolor drawings of fanciful foods, with make-believe recipes hand-lettered under each image by Warhol's mother—didn't have much impact: the *New York Times* called them "clever frivolity *in excelsis*."[21] Unable to find a publisher for an accompanying book of recipes and drawings, Warhol self-published it, but nobody wanted copies.

His inability to break through into the world of fine art (and accompanying fame) depressed Warhol. He later claimed he had a nervous breakdown in 1959 and through half of 1960.

Although Warhol wasn't always beloved by art critics or art buyers, he developed a following very early on. Among his admirers was his pet dachshund, Archie, shown here with Warhol in 1973.

Pop Art Arrives

Johns and Rauschenberg's new movement had a name: Pop Art. It had really begun in London in the mid-1950s. One textbook describes it this way: "The Pop artist turns outward to his environment—not to the natural environment, but the artificial one of mass popular culture—finding his material in the manipulated and programmed folkways and the mass-produced commodities of modern urban and suburban life." Pop Art, in a reversal from the traditional view, "accepts and approves the art (such as illustration and comic strips) and artifacts of mall culture as entirely valid art in themselves."[22]

Warhol loved the new art, but he had to find his own subjects and technique. He did a series of black-and-white paintings of sections of cheap advertisements. Then he did a series of paintings of blown-up comic strip characters such as Dick Tracy and Popeye. Then, in the summer of 1960, he tried a realistic, black-and-white picture of a Coke bottle, about six feet tall. He also painted a Coke bottle with elements of Abstract Expressionism. De Antonio told him he should destroy the Abstract Expressionist version and show the other one. "It's our society, it's who we are, it's absolutely beautiful," he said.[23]

While trying to transform his art, Warhol transformed himself. He wore silver-blond wigs, uncombed and not quite straight. He took to mumbling short, not-always coherent replies to questions. He exaggerated his limp wrists and the mincing way he walked—the "swish" mannerisms to which Johns and Rauschenberg objected. According to his biographer Bockris, this personal style, which became iconic, combined Marlon Brando and

Marilyn Monroe and served as a defensive strategy: no one could make fun of him, because he had already made fun of himself.

Ivan Karp, the assistant to Leo Castelli, came to look at the new paintings and told Warhol the only ones he thought mattered were the cold, straightforward ones like the Coke bottle. He took some slides back to the gallery because he thought some people who were interested in another new painter, Roy Lichtenstein, might be interested in Warhol. Karp brought a few collectors to Warhol's studio, and he sold a few paintings—though for far less than he could make for any commercial assignment.

Lichtenstein was also working with comic book images—but his paintings were far more powerful. Karp had no luck trying to get gallery owners to show Warhol's work. Some didn't like the work; others didn't like Warhol. "He was about the most colossal creep I had ever seen in my life," one said later.[24]

Leo Castelli was among those without interest. He didn't think he could show both Warhol and Lichtenstein: the works were similar, but Lichtenstein's were better. "You're mistaken," Warhol told him. "What I'm doing will be very different from what anybody else is doing . . . You will take me. I'll be back."[25]

Without a gallery, Warhol showed his paintings wherever he could, once putting a handful in a department store window behind mannequins wearing the latest spring dresses and hats. Then, late in 1961, Warhol told interior designer Muriel Latow that he was desperate. "Muriel, you've got fabulous ideas. Can't you give me an idea?"[26]

Latow said that she could, but it would cost him $50. He paid. She told him that since what he really liked most in the world was money, he should paint pictures of money.

Warhol thought that was a great idea. And then she told him he should paint "something you see every day and something that everybody would recognize. Something like a can of Campbell's Soup."

"Oh!" said Warhol. "That sounds fabulous!"[27]

3
Factory Setting

W hile his soup cans were being shown in Los Angeles, Warhol was turning out canvas after canvas in New York: Coke bottles, coffee cans, S & H Green Stamps, and more Campbell's Soup cans. He began experimenting with repetition and also with a new technique, silkscreening.

While Warhol's work helped him break into the New York art scene, it was his studio, the Factory, that helped him develop his work and his following among other artists.

WARHOL'S SILKSCREENING

Warhol's silkscreens began with a photograph. The photo was sent to a commercial silkscreen shop, where the image was projected onto silk (or a silk-like fabric) that had been stretched over a frame and coated with an emulsion that hardened when exposed to light. Where it wasn't exposed to light, it could be washed off, leaving clean fabric.

Back in the studio, Warhol or an assistant would lay the screen on a canvas, apply paint or printer's ink, and then push a rubber squeegee across it, forcing the paint through those areas not blocked by the hardened emulsion.

Sometimes the canvas was hand-painted in advance with solid-color backgrounds or spots of color to define, say, lipstick or eye shadow on a portrait. Occasionally, Warhol would paint over top of the silkscreened image, but usually the colors came first.[1]

Drawing on his collection of celebrity pictures, Warhol did silkscreen paintings of Elvis Presley, Troy Donahue, Warren Beatty, and Natalie Wood. Then, upon hearing the news that Marilyn Monroe had committed suicide (on August 4, 1962, the same day his *Campbell's Soup Cans* show closed), he did a series of portraits of her, using a publicity photograph taken by Gene Korman for the 1953 movie *Niagara*. He painted in the background, painted her eye shadow, lips, and face, and then applied the silkscreened image. In all, he did twenty-three paintings. The colors were garish, and often didn't line up properly

Warhol's silkscreened images of Marilyn Monroe became some of his most iconic works. Even today, fans flock to museums to view the original paintings up close and in person.

with the photographic image (they were "off register"). The most famous is known as the Marilyn diptych: 100 repetitions of her face across twelve feet of canvas.

Warhol's creativity exploded. He silkscreened all the paintings he had done earlier that summer, from Coke bottles to soup cans. He turned a lurid tabloid headline, "129 DIE IN JET!," and accompanying photograph into a painting by projecting the image onto a canvas and then painting over it. In three months, he painted a hundred pictures. By the end of 1962, he would paint 2,000—and he finally had a New York gallery in which to show his work.

A Gallery, at Last

Eleanor Ward, who owned the Stable Gallery, had been forced to cancel an exhibition scheduled for November. Instead, she decided to show Warhol, whose "incredible collection" of work had "absolutely stupefied" her.[2]

Just before that exhibition, Warhol had three paintings in a group Pop Art show at the Sidney Janis Gallery. Pop Art was the talk of the art world . . . and a week later, Warhol's show opened.

Running from November 6 to 24, 1962, it featured eighteen works, including some of the Marilyn Monroes, his *Do It Yourself* paintings (which looked like half-completed paint-by-number pictures), *129 Die in Jet!*, and his serial images of Campbell's Soup cans. This time, everyone noticed. Michael Fried wrote in *Art International* magazine that, at his best in the Marilyn Monroe paintings, Warhol "had . . . a feeling for what is truly human and pathetic in one of the exemplary myths of our time that I for one find moving."[3]

There was nothing else like it. It sold out even as people joked about how terrible it was. William Seitz bought a Marilyn Monroe for the Museum of Modern Art for $250. When one of his colleagues called him and said of the show, "Isn't it the most ghastly thing you've ever seen in your life?" Seitz answered, "Yes, isn't it. I bought one."[4]

The Public Face of Pop

Partly because of his art, partly because of his own odd appearance and behavior (he spent most of the opening and the after-party standing in a corner, barely mumbling

Among the celebrities Warhol chose to immortalize in silkscreen were Marilyn Monroe, Jackie Kennedy, Warren Beatty, Natalie Wood, and Elvis Presley (seen here).

when people spoke to him), Warhol became the primary target for everyone who wanted to attack Pop Art. But every attack only enhanced his fame.

It wasn't just Abstract Expressionists or critics who hated his art—so did many of his friends and his family. Warhol professed not to care. He said his philosophy was, "Don't think about making art, just get it done. Let everyone else decide whether it's good or bad, whether they love it or hate it. While they're deciding, make even more art."[5]

He began to cultivate what would become his life-long lifestyle, going out to openings, dinner, or parties every night. For him, parties weren't just about fun, they were part of the work of maintaining the image of the celebrity known as Andy Warhol.

During the summer of 1963, Warhol painted several of his most famous portraits, including a series of six-foot-tall silver images of Elvis Presley holding a gun. He hired a new assistant, Gerard Malanga, to help him with his silkscreens. Nathan Gluck continued to assist him on his commercial work, which he still relied on to pay the bills.

One series of paintings, related to *129 Die in Jet!*, was based on images of violence: car crashes, suicides, an electric chair. (He always denied he intended any social commentary; he said he simply found the images interesting.) He silkscreened newspaper photographs onto canvases covered with garish colors, and gave the paintings names like *Vertical Orange Car Crash* or *Lavender Disaster.* He put his creativity into the concept and design. Once he had decided what the piece should look like, it took only four minutes to complete. At that speed, mistakes were inevitable, but Warhol saw the mistakes as part of the art. As he famously told *TIME* magazine, "Paintings are too hard. Machines have less problems. I'd like to be a machine, wouldn't you?"[6]

In 2013, one of these paintings, *Silver Car Crash (Double Disaster)* sold at auction at Sotheby's for $104.5 million, the highest price ever paid at auction for a piece by Warhol.[7] Yet at the time, very few people wanted the grisly works. As a result, Warhol staged no solo exhibitions in New York in 1963, despite the success of his 1962 show.

The Birth of the Factory

Warhol's new space was a single room with a concrete floor and crumbling brick walls, about 100 feet long and forty feet wide, with four metal pillars supporting the low ceiling. A former hat factory, it was about to become a factory again: the Factory, one of the most famous locations in the New York art world.

The first things produced there were some of Warhol's most famous works: 400 sculptures of grocer boxes for Campbell's tomato juice, Kellogg's Cornflakes, Del Monte peach halves, Brillo Pads and other products, made out of plywood and silkscreened to look as much like the originals as possible.

Warhol sits in his studio in 1964, surrounded by dozens of his silkscreened images of celebrities, including his iconic paintings of Jacqueline Kennedy.

THE JACKIE KENNEDY PORTRAITS

On November 22, 1963, President John F. Kennedy was assassinated by Lee Harvey Oswald in Dallas, Texas. Publicly, Warhol said, "It was just something that happened. It isn't for me to judge."[8] But artistically, he responded by taking eight newspaper photographs of Jackie Kennedy, the president's widow, from before and after the assassination, and turning them into paintings. He made more than 300 in all, each typically 20 inches by 16 inches, which could be arranged in various combinations to form larger, gridded compositions, such as the 16-panel work in blue and grey, shown in Europe, that critic Frank O'Hara called "absolutely moving and beautiful."[9]

Today the Jackie paintings range in price from $1.2 million for individual paintings to tens of millions of dollars for multiple-portrait sets.[10]

Eleanor Ward at the Stable Gallery, who had refused to show Warhol's paintings of violence, wasn't too excited about the idea of a show made up of boxes, but she was eventually convinced to stage Warhol's art. The sculptures would sell for $300 to $600 each, Warhol told her.

He and Malanga got to work on the new pieces. It took three months. Warhol described his typical schedule during this time: "We usually worked till around midnight, and then we'd go down to the Village . . . I'd get home around four in the morning, make a few phone calls . . . and then when it started to get light I'd take a Seconal, sleep for a couple of hours and be back at the Factory by early afternoon."[11]

While the work was underway, a twenty-one-year-old hairdresser and lighting designer named Billy Name started renovating the studio, all in silver. "Silver was the future, it was spacey," Warhol wrote. "Silver was also the past—the Silver Screen . . . silver was narcissism—mirrors were backed with silver."[12]

While Name worked on the Factory, a lot of his friends started coming, mostly flamboyantly gay amphetamine (speed) users. Warhol himself had started to take a legally prescribed amphetamine, one reason he needed to take Seconal, a sleeping pill, every night. However, although surrounded by heavy drug users throughout his life, he was never a heavy user himself.

Warhol changed the way he looked again, favoring a black leather jacket, tight black jeans, T-shirts, high-heeled boots, dark glasses, and (to match the décor) a silver wig.

In April 1964, just before Boxes opened at the Stable Gallery, Warhol had a disagreement with Philip Johnson, an architect who had commissioned murals from various artists, including Warhol, to decorate the outside of the American pavilion at the New York World's Fair that summer. Warhol created a twenty-foot-square black-and-white piece entitled *The Thirteen Most Wanted Men*, which made use of the mug shots of criminals. But on April 16, after objections to Warhol's work from the governor of New York (who thought it might be insulting to Italians because most of the wanted men were Italian), Johnson told Warhol he had just twenty-four hours to replace or remove it.

Warhol silkscreened twenty-five identical images of Robert Moses, the city's planner and president of the Fair, to replace *The Thirteen Most Wanted Men,* but Johnson rejected that idea. Finally, Warhol simply ordered the panels to be painted silver.

"In one way I was glad the mural was gone: now I wouldn't have to feel responsible if one of the criminals ever got turned in to the FBI because someone had recognized him from my pictures," Warhol wrote later. He turned the silkscreens of the wanted criminals into paintings, noting that they "certainly weren't going to get caught from the kind of exposure they'd get at the Factory."[13]

Boxes

Warhol's Boxes show opened at the Stable Gallery on April 21. It looked like the interior of a warehouse with boxes of canned goods turning the gallery into a maze. The same day, Warhol held a party at the Factory. White, red, and green spotlights lit up the silver that covered everything—aluminum foil on the walls, ceiling, and

By 1980, when this photo was taken, Warhol was more than simply an artist. He was a celebrity in his own right, attracting actors, artists, and musicians to his Factory and becoming a fixture in New York's nightlife scene.

pipes, silver paint on the floor and everything else, right down to the toilet bowl. Rock music blasted.

According to Victor Bockris, the party marked a turning point in Warhol's career. It was the last time he was photographed in a group with the other famous Pop artists like Lichtenstein. "From now on he would only appear surrounded by his own people. It marked a removal from the pop-art world in general," Bockris wrote.[14] Warhol was moving away from being famous as an artist and toward being simply famous.

Famous, but not rich. Few of the boxes sold. Still, it was a successful show, as Warhol soon moved to the Leo Castelli Gallery, where he'd wanted to be since the Jasper Johns show several years earlier.

Meanwhile, the Factory had become the place to be. David Bourdon described it this way: "The place functioned as a combination clubhouse, community center, lounge, and cruising area for some of New York's more outlandish types—preening fashion models, ranting amphetamine heads, sulky poets, underground moviemakers, and imperious magazine editors, as well as wide-eyed college students and occasional movie personalities and rock star . . . Soon, professional photographers from all over the Western world were also hanging around the Factory, the new frontier of artistic far-outness."[15]

Poets did readings there. Actors put on plays. There were always parties. Warhol shot his films there. But somehow, he also managed to create art. His first show at Castelli's, in November of 1964, featured paintings of flowers, based on a color photo of hibiscus blossoms, taken by Patricia Caulfield, which he had seen in a magazine. (Caulfield eventually sued Warhol for using her photograph without permission, and after a long, costly court case, Warhol agreed to give her several paintings, and a percentage of all profits from future reproductions, in payment. After that, for fear of being sued again, Warhol mostly took his own photographs.)

In a marked contrast to his previous few shows, the flower paintings sold out. *Newsweek* profiled Warhol. The critics were generally positive about the paintings. As always, though, they were ambivalent toward Warhol himself, whose primary focus increasingly seemed to be his own fame.

Controversies added to his image. Warhol had several solo exhibitions outside the United States in 1965. One in Toronto, scheduled to open on March 18, attracted controversy when Charles F. Comfort, the director of the National Gallery of Canada, refused to certify that the boxes were works of art. As a result, they were subject to a duty of 20 percent—$60 on each of the $300 boxes, eighty of which were being brought in for the show.

As usual, Warhol expressed indifference. "It really doesn't matter much to me—I don't care much," he told the *Globe and Mail* newspaper.[16]

Warhol Retires

In May of that year, Warhol made his first trip to Europe since becoming famous, for the opening of an exhibit of his flower paintings at the Sonnabend Gallery in Paris. The show broke attendance records. French critics praised Warhol. And then Warhol dropped a bombshell: he told the French press that he was retiring from painting to make films.

According to Victor Bockris, the announcement was a carefully planned strategy to increase the prices of

With his sculptural boxes, designed to look exactly like the product packaging they copied, Warhol started a discussion about what constitutes art and why people value it more in some forms than others.

his paintings (the flower paintings were selling for only $2,000). Warhol figured if he stayed away from painting for a while, the prices would increase. As well, "Andy felt the pop-art explosion was spent."[17]

As a result, Warhol's next show at the Leo Castelli Gallery, April 2 to 27, 1966, was conceived as Warhol's "farewell to art."

Castelli's assistant, Karp, had suggested Warhol paint something "pastoral, like cows," so he wallpapered one room of the gallery with repeated images of a cow's head. He filled the second room with free-floating helium-filled silver pillows.

There were few sales. Warhol would not have another major show at Castelli's until 1977. He didn't care; he was turning his attention to film and music. What he produced would be just as revolutionary and controversial as his art.

4
Fifteen Minutes of Film Fame

Warhol had always been interested in movies, so his move into that medium wasn't too surprising. His decision was influenced by his friendship with Emile de Antonio, with whom he viewed a lot of experimental films at the Film-Maker's Co-op. In July 1963, Warhol bought an eight-millimeter movie camera for $1,200 and made his first film—five and a half hours of poet John Giorno (with whom he was involved at the time) sleeping. Much of the footage repeats, just like Warhol often repeated images in his static art. Black and white and silent, it was shot at the standard speed of a sound film—twenty-four frames per second—but projected at the silent-film speed of sixteen frames per second, which meant that not only was it a film of someone sleeping, it was a film of someone sleeping *in slow motion*.

"*Sleep* begins with a 20-minute scene of Giorno's belly," writes Lavanya Ramanathan of the *Washington Post*. "Followed by Giorno on his back. Then there is some quality time with Giorno's armpit. Then something else—perhaps a knee?" Unlike in real life, Ramanathan notes, "no one ever complains they just didn't get enough *Sleep*."[1]

The news that Warhol had made a movie triggered all kinds of publicity. "It was absurd," Girono said later.

"He was on the cover of *Film Culture* and *Harper's Bazaar* before the movie was finished!"[2]

The film premiered on January 17, 1964, at the Gramercy Arts Theater. It was a benefit screening for the Film-Makers' Co-op, but it couldn't have been much of one—only nine people attended and two of them left during the first hour. At first the Los Angeles debut seemed more promising—about 500 people turned out at the Cinema Theatre—but fifteen minutes into the film, the first people walked out. Not long after that, they began walking out and asking for their money back, despite the "No refunds" sign. The theater manager finally agreed to give out free passes for another show and handed out

Always fascinated by Hollywood, Warhol finally ventured into moving pictures in the 1960s. Unlike the Hollywood films he admired, though, Warhol shot more experimental movies while exploring the medium.

more than 200. By the time the film dragged to its close, only fifty people were left.

Warhol's second film was *Andy Warhol Films Jack Smith Filming Normal Love*. Smith was a controversial underground filmmaker who would appear as an actor in several other Warhol films, as would many of his actors. "I picked something up from him for my own movies— the way he used anyone who happened to be around that day, and also how he just kept shooting until the actors got bored," Warhol said.[3]

One of Smith's actors, Taylor Mead, accompanied Warhol and others in late September of 1963 on a cross-country car trip to the opening of the Elvis exhibit at the Ferus Gallery in Los Angeles. While there, Warhol filmed scenes for another film, *Tarzan and Jane Regained . . . Sort of*, featuring Mead and actress Naomi Levine.

Levine was the first person to appear naked in an Andy Warhol film. She wouldn't be the last.

Let the Cameras Roll

For the next few years, Warhol was always filming something. (Eventually, there would be well over 200 films.) His next "major" film after *Sleep* was *Kiss*, which featured a series of couples posing in a mouth-to-mouth kiss for three minutes without moving. The scenes were originally shown as individual segments, one a week. *Haircut* was like *Sleep*, only it featured a haircut. It was also much shorter. *Eat* featured a man eating a mushroom.

Warhol said he made these films the way he did, with a stationary camera focused on a single actor doing the same thing over a long period of time, because "here at last is a chance to look only at the star for as long as you like," he said. "It was also easier to make,"[4] he added.

Jonas Mekas, a pioneer avant-garde filmmaker, a founder of Anthology Film Archives, and an early supporter and presenter of Warhol's films, said, "You watch a Warhol film without being hurried . . . The camera hardly moves from the spot. It remains focused on the subject as if there were nothing more beautiful and important than this subject. We can look at it longer than we are accustomed to . . . We begin to understand that we have never really seen what happens when hair is cut or how one eat . . . The whole reality of our environment suddenly becomes interesting in a new way."[5]

Soon Warhol decided to take the same approach to filming a much more monumental subject. Filmed on the night of July 25 to 26 from 8:06 p.m. to 2:42 a.m., *Empire* is a single static shot of the Empire State Building. The film begins with a totally white screen. As the sun sets, the image of the building emerges. Floodlights come on. Interior lights flicker on and off for the next six and a half hours. Then the floodlights go off, and the remainder of the film takes place in, essentially, total darkness.

At the premiere, people walked out, booed, and threw paper cups at the screen. In Malanga's words, "*Empire* was a movie where nothing happened except how the audience reacted."[6]

Mary Woronov, who appeared in Warhol's later films, said in 2008 that it took her forty years to realize Warhol wasn't doing a film, he was doing a painting. "Pop art put the image back in painting and Andy took it even further and put the image on film instead of canvas...these films were never meant to screen in a theater, where I thought they were boring. They were meant to hang on a wall. They are Andy's greatest paintings."[7]

From early 1964 through November of 1966, Warhol shot some 500 *Screen Tests*. Visitors to the Factory were seated in front of a camera on a tripod and asked to be as still as possible and not blink while the camera was running.

The subjects ran from various Factory denizens to celebrities such as poet Allen Ginsberg and musicians Bob Dylan, Lou Reed, and David Bowie. Some of the footage was compiled into longer films with titles like *The 13 Most Beautiful Boys*, *The 13 Most Beautiful Women*, *50 Fantastics*, and *50 Personalities*. In 1966, Warhol and his assistant, Gerard Malanga, put together a book featuring *Screen Test* stills of 17 women and 37 men, along with Malanga's poetry. Called *Screen Tests/A Diary*, it was published by Kulchur Press in 1967.

Warhol's Superstars

Warhol tended to use the same people over and over in his films. They became what he called "superstars," although in general he paid them nothing for their work; they did it just to be part of the Factory scene, and because he kept promising them that someday they really would be superstars.

Warhol's first "superstar" to attract media attention was Jane Holzer, nicknamed Baby Jane. Holzer was introduced to Warhol by a friend. Warhol asked if she'd like to be in a movie he was making called *Soap Opera*.

Soap Opera, the first film Holzer starred in for Warhol, was the first Warhol film to be mentioned in the *New York Times*.

After becoming a celebrity, Warhol went on to make celebrities—or "superstars." His first big star was model and actress Jane Holzer, nicknamed Baby Jane.

Holzer eventually appeared in several Warhol movies and also allowed Warhol to escort her to parties, gallery openings, and rock shows, which attracted a lot of press attention, much to Warhol's delight. She tended to avoid the Factory, though; she didn't like the drug use there.

Poor Little Rich Girl

Hundreds of people appeared in Warhol's more than 200 films. The most famous of his superstars was Edie Sedgwick.

Sedgwick began hanging out regularly at the Factory in March of 1965. During one of those visits, Warhol put her into his movie *Vinyl*. After that she starred in *Poor Little Rich Girl*, which consisted of her lying on her bed, talking on the phone, and showing off her clothes, explaining how she had spent her entire inheritance in just half a year.

Warhol started taking Sedgwick everywhere. They were photographed with Lady Bird Johnson, the wife of President Lyndon Johnson, at the opening of a show called Three Centuries of American Painting at the Metropolitan Museum of Art. And when Warhol went to Paris for the opening of his show at the Sonnabend Gallery that April, he took Sedgwick with him. When he got back, he asked his scriptwriter, Ron Tavel, to write a script for Sedgwick to star in. "Something in a kitchen. White and clean and plastic," was his direction. The resulting film was called, not too surprisingly, *Kitchen*. In it, three people sit around a table in a small kitchen, talking about nothing in particular. Most of the dialogue can't even be heard. At the end, Sedgwick's character is killed for no apparent reason.

Famous novelist Norman Mailer proclaimed that the film "captured the essence of every boring, dead day one's ever had in a city . . . I suspect that a hundred years from now people will look at *Kitchen* and say, 'Yes, that is the way it was in the late Fifties, early Sixties in America.'"[8]

Kitchen was the last film Ron Tavel wrote for Warhol. Chuck Wein pushed him out, and was credited as writer and assistant director on the next film starring Sedgwick, *Beauty No. 2*, in which she sits in her underwear on her bed alongside a man in jockey shorts, drinking vodka

While Baby Jane was Warhol's first "superstar," his biggest star was Edie Sedgwick. The young actress starred in a number of Warhol's films before her sudden death in 1971.

while being questioned off camera by Wein. Through the course of the film, she gradually falls apart emotionally.

When *Beauty No. 2* premiered on July 17, some critics compared Edie Sedgwick to Marilyn Monroe. That excited Warhol, who thought she could be his ticket to the big time of movie making.

But as Sedgwick's fame grew, people outside Warhol's circle began telling her she no longer needed him, and Sedgwick left the Factory in February 1966.

Her final film (not a Warhol film), *Ciao! Manhattan*, tells the story of young Susan Superstar as she parties her way through Manhattan as a Warhol superstar. Set in the character's parents' mansion in Southern California, its story is told through a series of flashbacks comprising film footage from a previous, unrealized project. Combining scripted segments with audio interviews carried out while Sedgwick was high on drugs, it ends with the headlines announcing the real-life Sedgwick's death in 1971.

The Velvet Underground

Warhol's films changed a bit when Paul Morrissey, a former social worker who hated to be around drugs and was very much a film traditionalist, emerged as Warhol's right-hand man. He wanted to make commercial films and managed to convince Warhol that his own films could be profitable.

Morrissey also looked for ways to market Warhol's name. In mid-December of 1965, he convinced theater producer Michael Myerberg to call his new discotheque Andy Warhol's Up, and said Warhol could also provide the music.

RON TAVEL: WARHOL'S "SCREENWRITER"

Once Warhol started making movies with sound, he needed dialogue. He had seen Ronnie Tavel at a poetry reading, and invited him to the Factory to sit in a chair off-camera and talk while he shot his first movie with sound, *Harlot*, starring Mario Montez.

Tavel continued to write "scenarios" for several months. His films included *The Life of Juanita Castro*, *Horse*, *Vinyl*, *Hedy*, and *Kitchen*.

A description of how *Horse* was filmed indicates just how little a "script" for a Warhol film had in common with a standard Hollywood screenplay:

"Tavel's task in the case of *Horse* was to get 66 minutes of film footage from four unprepared and intimidated young men . . . and a horse. To accomplish it, Tavel devised a scheme in which he wrote the names of the actors on four placards and all the action and lines of dialogue on what he called cheat sheets. These latter were ordered in some semblance of a plot and would be held up in sequence by Warhol's assistant Gerard Malanga on cue from Tavel, who moved about the periphery of the set and held up the placard bearing the name of one of the four actors, chosen in accordance with how he saw the story evolving. Seeing his name on Tavel's cue card, the designated actor would turn to Malanga and read his line."[9]

That meant, of course, that Warhol needed to find a band, and as it happened, one had recently presented itself: the Velvet Underground, led by singer/guitarist/songwriter Lou Reed. Warhol heard them play, and afterward met with Reed and invited them to the Factory.

Shortly thereafter, a singer/actress named Nico returned to New York and got in touch with Warhol's assistant, Gerard Malanga. Warhol proposed adding her to the Velvet Underground. She would be his next superstar.

First, of course, he had to convince the Velvet Underground that they needed Nico. She wanted a back-up band, and they had no interest in being a back-up band. But Warhol was offering to manage them, give them a place to rehearse, finance their equipment,

Warhol (*center*) with the Velvet Underground. Warhol briefly managed the New York rock band, producing and designing some of their most famous albums.

support them, and make them famous—in return for twenty-five percent of their earnings.

In the end, the band agreed to Morrissey's suggestion that Nico sing some songs, but not all. It helped that Nico was quite taken with Lou Reed and Reed was taken with Warhol. They even agreed to change the name of the band to the Velvet Underground and Nico.

The Velvet Underground performed as part of a week of mixed-media shows Warhol presented in February at the Film-Makers' Cinematheque. Called *Andy Warhol Uptight*, and intended as a kind of dress rehearsal for the new disco, it featured the Velvet Underground and Nico performing while the Warhol films *Vinyl*, *Empire*, and *Eat* ran in the background. A new film, *More Milk, Yvette*, was premiered. While the band played, a group of interpretive dancers pretended to shoot up heroin, whip each other, and perform crucifixions.

That same month, Warhol appeared on TV and officially announced he was sponsoring the Velvet Underground.

Andy Warhol Uptight never played Andy Warhol's Up; the manager there changed his mind. Instead, it morphed into the *Exploding Plastic Inevitable*, which first played a dance hall called the Dom. Warhol himself ran the film and slide projectors and changed the light filters, essentially conducting everything that happened.

Press reactions to what may have been the first multi-media show staged in New York were good, and it came just when Warhol's "farewell to art" show opened at Castelli's.

It looked like he'd made the right decision to "retire" from painting. His film *My Hustler* had just opened and become the first Warhol film to make a profit. The

Exploding Plastic Inevitable brought in $18,000 in its first week. Warhol had started working on the Velvet Underground and Nico album.

Morrissey handed over management of the *Exploding Plastic Inevitable* to booking agent Charlie Rothchild, who took the whole show on the road to Los Angeles . . . where it promptly fell apart, done in by internal disagreements and a fierce rivalry between the East and West Coast music scenes. Warhol returned to New York. The *Exploding Plastic Inevitable* would continue to tour, minus Warhol and others, for several months.

Chelsea Girls

Warhol's financial situation suddenly turned sour: the Velvet Underground experiment had lost money. Though his lifestyle made it hard for people to believe, Warhol was making less money in the 1960s than he had as a commercial artist in the 1950s.

Warhol had discovered, after being commissioned to do a portrait entitled *Edith Scull 36 Times*, that painting portraits was an easy, reliable way to make money. That summer he did a few more to finance the rest of his activities. For the rest of his career, his portraits—silkscreened photographs over pre-painted canvasses—would be a major source of his income.

Over three months, beginning in mid-June of 1966, Warhol shot fifteen one- and two-reel films. They had no plots (or even scripts). They were shot in one take, until the reels, thirty-five minutes long, ran out. Warhol liked the idea of simply pointing the camera at people and waiting for something to happen. But this put a lot of pressure on the performers, most of whom were already on drugs.

Warhol and Morrissey would feed the actors nasty rumors ahead of time, playing them against one another. The resulting "performances" were raw, sometimes violent, very real—and led to many of the performers despising each other in real life.

THE VELVET UNDERGROUND & NICO

In March 1967, MGM released the Velvet Underground's album, *The Velvet Underground and Nico*. Production was delayed partly because of the Warhol-designed cover, which featured a banana that could be peeled. The album didn't do well at the time, although it still sells steadily today. Newspapers and magazines wouldn't carry any ads for it, since some of the songs dealt with controversial subjects like drug use. Most radio stations wouldn't play it. In fact, the reaction was so negative that lead singer Lou Reed didn't play in New York again until 1970. He also began looking for a new manager.

Worse (from Warhol's point of view): The album didn't make any money.

Reviewing the footage, Warhol and Morrissey realized the films could be made to relate to each other, and assembled twelve of them into a six-and-a-half-hour film called *Chelsea Girls*. Because of the length, Warhol decided to show two reels side by side on a split screen, with sound coming from only one side at a time. Some of the films were color. Some were black-and-white. The overall effect, at least for some people, was mesmerizing.

Chelsea Girls cost just $1,500 to $3,000 to make and grossed $130,000 in its first nineteen weeks in New York.

In 1966, Warhol shot the movie *Chelsea Girls* at his Factory. Although the film was six and a half hours long and shown on a split screen, it would become one of Warhol's most well-known films.

Several of its participants became famous: Ondine, Nico, International Velvet (Susan Bottomly), Brigid Berlin, and Mary Woronov. They even got paid a little: they were eventually given $1,000 each to sign a release.

A Hard Life at the Factory

Just before *Chelsea Girls* opened, one of the performers in the *Exploding Plastic Inevitable*, Danny Williams, committed suicide. When Williams's mother called the Factory, Warhol refused to speak to her. "I don't care," he said. "What a pain in the neck, he was just an amphetamine addict."[10]

Drugs and the constant in-fighting were taking their toll on many members of Warhol's Factory set. But Warhol pressed on making movies. He even made one starring his mother, Julia, filmed in her basement apartment.

Warhol's movie-making wasn't going smoothly, but at least he had a May trip to the Cannes Film Festival to show *Chelsea Girls* to look forward to. The three-week trip proved to be a disaster: *Chelsea Girls* was not shown. When Warhol got back to the States, he flew to a Velvet Underground concert in Boston with Paul Morrissey and Nico, only to find Lou Reed had hired a new manager. Nico wasn't permitted to sing. It was the end of Warhol's connection to the Velvet Underground.

In July 1967, the Hudson Theater started running Warhol's *My Hustler*. The film drew a decent audience, so the manager called up Paul Morrissey and asked him if they had anything else. He asked for a film like Warhol's *I, a Woman*. Warhol decided instead to shoot *I, a Man*, a feature-length comedy. Two other comedies followed, *Bikeboy* and *Nude Restaurant*.

But *I, a Man*'s most distinguishing feature is that it features Valerie Solanas. During the course of shooting, Solanas, a lesbian, allegedly told Warhol actress Ultra Violet that "love can only exist between two secure, freewheeling, groovy female females. Love is for chicks. Why do you let him exploit you? Why don't you sink a shiv into his chest?"[11]

With that attitude, it's not surprising Solanas headed up, and was the only member of, SCUM (the Society for Cutting Up Men), which called for the elimination of males in the interest of world peace.

Solanas failed to eliminate all males, but in 1968, she came very close to eliminating Andy Warhol.

5
Attacked by SCUM

W arhol found Valerie Solanas's performance honest and funny. But Solanas complained that talking to Warhol was "like talking to a chair."

Nico also appeared in *I, a Man*. Warhol had pushed her to record a solo album, but he was getting tired of her. She was on drugs and spending a lot of time with other celebrities—Jim Morrison, Bob Dylan, Brian Jones. She wasn't as focused on Andy as he wanted her to be.

Other things were changing. Paul Morrissey installed cubicles in the Factory to make it more businesslike. Warhol's long-time assistant, Gerard Malanga, left the Factory that summer and never really returned. Billy Name, who had created the Factory's silver look and managed the place like a theater, saw that Morrissey was taking over, and wondered when he would get anything more than the $10 a week and a place to live he'd been paid since he started.

Warhol Goes (Back) to College

That fall, Warhol started a tour of college campuses, with a program deliberately designed to annoy his audiences.

FINAL

DAILY ■ NEWS

NEW YORK'S PICTURE NEWSPAPER ®

 8¢ **10¢ OUTSIDE L.I. AND SUBURBS**

Vol. 49. No. 296 Copr. 1968 News Syndicate Co. Inc.   New York, N.Y. 10017, Tuesday, June 4, 1968★   WEATHER: Sunny and warm.

ACTRESS SHOOTS ANDY WARHOL

Cries 'He Controlled My Life'

NEWS photo by Jack Smith

Guest From London Shot With Pop Art Movie Man

Shot in attack on underground movie producer Andy Warhol, London art gallery owner Mario Amaya, about 30, walks to ambulance. Warhol was shot and critically wounded by one of his female stars, Valerie Solanas, 28, the "girl on the staircase" in one of his recent films. She walked into Andy's sixth-floor office at 33 Union Square West late yesterday afternoon and got off at least five shots. Valerie later surrenuered. See ➤   —*Stories on page 3*

NEWS photo by Tom Monaster

Warhol (r.) was doing his thing with friend in Village spot recently.

The morning after Valerie Solanas barged into the Factory and shot Warhol, the incident was front-page news in New York and across the country.

The students turned out to hear Warhol speak, and Warhol refused to say a word. Typically, he'd show a segment of the incredibly boring *The 24 Hour Movie* (also known as ****), then, as actress Viva described it, he "stood on the stage, blushing and silent, while Paul Morrissey, the professor, delivered a totally intellectual anti-intellectual rapid-paced fifteen minute mini-lecture putting down art films, hippies, and marijuana, saying things like 'At least heroin doesn't change your personality.' Then I . . . answered questions—'The reason we make these movies is because it's fun, especially the dirty parts'—and advised them to drop out of school. Then I would rant about everybody in authority."[1]

Students often responded by hissing and booing. Warhol got into even more trouble later in the year when he sent Allen Midgette to colleges in Utah and Oregon to impersonate him at public appearances. It took four months for anyone to notice. After that, he had to go to the colleges for real to make up for the deception.

According to New York disc jockey Terry Noel, "the hatred for Andy got real serious."[2]

Some of it came from his own people. His film *Imitation of Christ* was released in November—and withdrawn after one showing. The same thing happened with *The 24 Hour Movie*, which premiered in mid-December. Warhol's superstars were furious that films they'd worked on for a year, which Warhol had promised would make them famous, ended up simply being discarded.

Warhol and his superstars were getting attacked in the press, too. *TIME* art critic Robert Hughes wrote, "They were all cultural space-debris, drifting fragments from a variety of sixties subculture . . . if Warhol's superstar . . . had possessed talent, discipline, or stamina, they would not have needed him. But then, he would not have needed them. They gave him his ghostly aura of power."[3]

One positive event was the arrival of Frederick W. Hughes at the Factory. One thing he did right away was sell a lot of Warhol's earlier, mostly ignored paintings, like the death-and-disaster scenes. Then he started landing portrait commissions for Warhol, each one priced at $25,000.

For the first time, Warhol's art could actually pay his bills.

Hints of Violence

One night in November 1967, a friend of Ondine's, called Sammy the Italian, ran in with a gun, lined Warhol and others up on the couch, and told them he was going to play Russian roulette. He put the gun to Paul Morrissey's head and pulled the trigger. Nothing happened. Nico got up to leave, and he pointed at the ceiling and pulled the trigger again. This time it fired.

At one point, Sammy put a woman's plastic rain hat on Warhol's head, made him kneel on the floor, and said he was going to take a hostage. Actor Taylor Mead jumped him from behind, and after a struggle, Sammy ran away.

When the police arrived, they didn't take the attack seriously. Neither did the newspapers. The *New York Times* wasn't at all sure the attack had happened, and even if it had, said, "it wouldn't be an important story anyway."

"The real thud was that no one cared about us," said Billy Name.[4]

At the beginning of 1968, Warhol took his entourage to Arizona to film a movie called *Lonesome Cowboys*.

They didn't exactly fit in there, and simulated gang rape in the film led to an official complaint to the FBI, which placed Warhol under surveillance. They suspected he was about to commit the crime of interstate transportation of obscene material. They eventually concluded that no crime had been committed.

Back in New York, Warhol set about moving the Factory. But more changed than just the building. A new manager, Jed Johnson, replaced Gerard Malanga. And "the Silver Period was definitely over, we were into white now," Warhol wrote. "Also, the new Factory was definitely not a place where the old insanity could go on . . . the big desks up front as you came in off the elevator gave people the hint that there was something going on in the way of business, that it wasn't all just hanging around anymore."[5]

In part, the new more business-like Factory was a reaction to the Russian roulette incident, but Warhol couldn't escape his rather unstable circle of acquaintances that easily. In particular, he couldn't escape Valerie Solanas.

In an interview with the *Village Voice* that winter, Solanas called Warhol a "son of a b****" and said every word that came out of his mouth was a lie, but also claimed he was still planning to produce a script she had given him.[6]

In truth, the script she'd given him, just before he went to Cannes, had simply gone into a pile with everything else he received. When he got back from Cannes, Solanas asked for it back, and Warhol told her he'd lost it. She started calling regularly, demanding money. When she also started making threats, Warhol stopped taking her calls.

Meanwhile, very little new work was being produced. *Lonesome Cowboys* was still undeveloped and unedited.

SCUM MANIFESTO

In 1967, radical feminist and Warhol hanger-on Valerie Solanas published the *SCUM Manifesto*, a diatribe against men and a plea for the women of the world to fix the problems men had caused. While Solanas called for women to form a society that would rid the world of men once and for all, it is debated whether "SCUM" in the *SCUM Manifesto* really stands for "Society for Cutting Up Men." While that name appeared in an advertisement Solanas placed prior to release of her book, she later said that the group was not real, nor did she intend it to be; it was merely a literary device used to get people's attention. Either way, Solanas got what she wanted: the *SCUM Manifesto* has been reprinted ten times in English and has been translated into at least thirteen languages over the years.

Warhol let Paul Morrissey go ahead with a project called *The Surfing Movie* (or sometimes *San Diego Surf*). Warhol took his cast and crew out to La Jolla, California, and rented a mansion for a three-week shoot. The police kept a very close watch on them. Once again there was a great deal of friction on the set. Warhol himself was detached. The film was never released.

Back in New York, Valerie Solanas bought two guns.

Vengeance for Valerie Solanas

On Monday, June 3, 1968, Warhol spent the morning talking to Fred Hughes on the phone. Hughes had a frightening story of violence to tell Warhol: he'd been mugged the night before.

At 2:30 p.m., Valerie Solanas went to the Factory. She'd become convinced Warhol was conspiring against her with Maurice Giordias, publisher of Olympia Press, who had given her an advance of $600 to write a novel based on her *SCUM Manifesto*.

Told Warhol was out, she waited outside. When Warhol finally arrived at the Factory at 4:15 p.m., she joined him and Jed Johnson, who was carrying some fluorescent lights. They entered the building together. Warhol noticed that Solanas was wearing a thick turtleneck sweater under a trench coat, even though it was a hot summer day. She was also wearing makeup— something that, as a radical feminist, she never wore. She seemed on edge, and kept twisting a brown paper bag in her hands.

Up in the Factory, Hughes was writing a memo at his desk and Paul Morrissey was talking on the phone to Viva, who was having her hair done in preparation for a role in the film *Midnight Cowboy*. Meanwhile, Mario Amaya, an art critic and curator, was waiting for Warhol so he could discuss an upcoming retrospective in London.

When the elevator arrived, Morrissey went to the bathroom and handed the phone to Warhol. Johnson went into Warhol's private office. Warhol had just signaled Hughes to take the phone and carry on the conversation with Viva when Solanas pulled a .32 automatic from the paper bag. She fired a shot at Warhol but missed.

Viva, hearing it over the phone, thought someone had cracked a whip.

Warhol screamed, "No! No! Valerie! Don't do it!" but Solanas fired a second time. She missed again. Warhol flung himself on the floor and tried to crawl under a desk, but her third shot connected.

The bullet entered through his right side, tearing through his lung, then ricocheting through his esophagus, gall bladder, liver, spleen, and intestines before exiting his left side, leaving a large hole. He felt "a horrible, horrible pain, like a cherry bomb exploding inside me."[7]

Thinking she'd killed him, Solanas fired her fourth shot at Amaya, who was crouching on the floor. She missed. She fired again, this time hitting him slightly above the hip; the bullet went through him without damaging any organs, though it missed his spine by only a quarter of an inch. He ran into the back room and threw his body against the doors to hold them shut.

Solanas then pointed the gun at Hughes. He begged her not to shoot him. She walked over to the elevator and pressed the button, then returned and aimed the gun at his forehead. She pulled the trigger, but the gun jammed. She pulled a second gun, a .22 caliber, from the brown paper bag, but then the elevator arrived. Instead of shooting Hughes, she left.

Hughes called an ambulance and the police.

It took half an hour for the ambulance to arrive. It delivered Warhol to the emergency room of Columbus Hospital at 4:45 p.m. The doctors had no idea who he was. But they did know he was in a bad way. At 4:51 p.m., Warhol was pronounced clinically dead, but Amaya, who was on the table across the room, sat up and screamed, "Don't you know who this is? It's Andy Warhol. He's

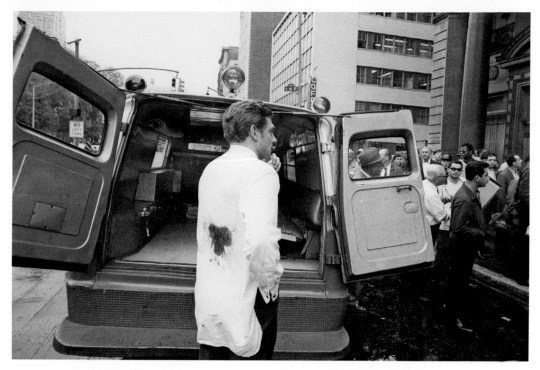

Moments after Valerie Solanas shot Warhol, Warhol's associate, Mario Amaya, also wounded in the struggle, walks out onto the street to a waiting ambulance.

famous. And he's rich. He can afford to pay for an operation . . . do something!"[8]

Warhol was "dead" for ninety seconds while the doctors cut open his chest and massaged his heart. When it restarted, they began to operate, removing his ruptured spleen and working to repair as much damage as they could. The operation took five and a half hours.

While Warhol was on the operating table, Solanas surrendered to a rookie traffic cop named William Shemalix, handing over the guns and telling him she had shot Warhol "because he had too much control of my life."[9]

With her arrest, Fred Hughes and Jed Johnson, who had been held for questioning, were released.

The Aftermath

The shooting shocked Warhol's family. Malanga took the subway to Warhol's townhouse after the shooting. Julia let him in. He was just in time to intercept a phone call from someone who had heard the news on the radio. After he hung up, he told Julia that Andy had been hurt and he was going to take her to the hospital. When she found out just how badly he'd been hurt, she wept, "My little Andy, they hurt my little Andy." Because of her own poor heart condition, hospital attendants put her in a wheelchair and took her to a private room.[10]

While Julia Warhola prayed for her "little Andy," his brother Paul was told by the doctor that there was only a fifty-fifty chance Warhol would pull through. Later, his other brother, John, would say he didn't realize how famous Andy was until he was shot and he saw all the headlines.

But the headlines were short-lived; even Warhol's knack for publicity had failed him. The night after Warhol was shot in New York, Robert Kennedy was shot in Los Angeles after winning the California primary. Warhol was relegated to the inside pages.

Kennedy died, but Warhol lived.

On June 13, Warhol's doctors reported he was on his way to a complete recovery. Meanwhile, Solanas was sent for psychiatric evaluation. On June 28, she was indicted on charges of attempted murder, assault, and illegal possession of a gun. Her bail was set at $10,000.

Warhol would remain in the hospital throughout June and July. While he was there, Ultra Violet asked him, "How do you explain it all? Why were you the one to get shot?"

BAD PRESS

Many of the press accounts following Warhol's shooting were unsympathetic variations on the theme that "he had it coming."

***TIME*'s story, "Felled by SCUM," was downright brutal. It began, "Americans who deplore crime and disorder might consider the case of Andy Warhol, who for years has celebrated every form of licentiousness . . . the pop-art king was the blond guru of a nightmare world, photographing depravity and calling it truth. He surrounded himself with freakily named people . . . playing games of lust, perversion, drug addiction and brutality before his crotchety cameras. Last week one of his grotesque bit players made the game quite real."[12]**

"I was in the wrong place at the right time," he answered.[11]

Just about a year after the shooting, in June of 1969, Solanas was sentenced to three years in prison. Since she'd already served one, she'd be out in two more. Lou Reed complained that "You get more for stealing a car" and thought "the hatred directed towards [Warhol] by society was obviously reflected in the judgment."

But John Warhola said the police told his brother that Solanas would go to jail for a long time if he appeared in court to testify against her. He chose not to because he was still recuperating.

Although famous for hating men in general, Valerie Solanas's reasons for shooting Warhol were far less philosophical: she was mad because he wouldn't produce a film she had pitched him.

Warhol was sent home on July 28, 1968. He spent his fortieth birthday in bed. But by August, Warhol, though weak, was back at work, painting a commissioned multiple portrait of Margaretta "Happy" Rockefeller, wife of the governor of New York. He appeared in public again for the first time on September 4.

"Since I was shot everything is such a dream to me. I don't know whether or not I'm really alive—whether I died," he said. And, he added, "I'm afraid. I don't understand why. I am afraid of God alone, and I wasn't before."[13]

6
Retirement, Cut Short

S ome things at the Factory had continued without Warhol. Paul Morrissey was more in charge of the filmmaking operation than ever before. He'd shot the movie *Flesh* while Warhol was in the hospital. It cost $4,000 and ran for six months at the Garrick Theatre, and gained its star, Joe Dallesandro, a cult following. It also got better reviews than many Warhol films—possibly because Morrissey directed it, although Morrissey played down his involvement.

In October 1969, Warhol was able to shoot another movie himself, eventually known as *Blue Movie*. It got its title not only because it contained explicit sex, but also because Warhol accidentally shot it indoors on outdoor film, which gave it a bluish tinge.

Meanwhile, a series of tape recordings Warhol had done with Ondine in 1965 and 1967 were being transcribed for a book to capitalize on his shooting. Called *a: A Novel*, the book was published by Grove Press in November. The reviews were bad.

In December, Warhol almost fainted when he answered the phone and heard Valerie Solanas on the other end. She wished him a Merry Christmas, then said she'd shoot him again if he didn't meet her demands: she wanted to be

Although the shooting by Valerie Solanas changed Warhol's life, he was nearly back to his old self six months later, when this photo was taken.

on Johnny Carson's *Tonight Show*, she wanted her *SCUM Manifesto* published in the *Daily News*, and she wanted $25,000 in cash. As a result of that call, and her threats against others, she was locked away again and her bail increased, eventually, to $100,000. She would remain in jail until the sentencing in June.

Andy Gets Lost

Warhol seemed a bit lost in 1969, as though trying to figure out what to do next. *Blue Movie* opened on July 21, but instead of being the huge success Warhol hoped it would be, it was seized for being obscene. And far from generating respect, it got reviews like Rex Reed's. "Warhol is merely a joke now," Reed wrote. "He has contributed nothing of any real significance to the contemporary cinema."[1]

That fall, Warhol started an underground movie magazine called *Interview*. It didn't make much of an impact at the time, but it would become a major part of his business in the 1970s.

The year ended with Warhol and Morrissey making their most expensive ($20,000 to $30,000)—and most successful—movie thus far: *Trash*, starring Joe Dallesandro and, as his wife, the female impersonator Holly Woodlawn. Instead of being about sex, it was about drugs.

The actors earned $25 a day. *Trash* eventually grossed $1.5 million. Warhol hoped to repeat the success with *Women in Revolt*, his next film, but when it finally opened in 1972, even though it got good reviews, it didn't make nearly as much money.

Warhol poses with some of his lesser-known superstars. While Edie Sedgwick and Baby Jane would go on to become household names, others, like Joe Dallesandro and Holly Woodlawn, were cult favorites.

In 1970, an international travelling retrospective of Warhol's work was planned, but Warhol gave the appearance of not being very interested. "I like empty walls," he said. "As soon as you put something on them they look terrible."[2]

STICKY FINGERS

Although Warhol's experiment with the music industry hadn't gone as planned, with the Velvet Underground eventually dropping him and the *Exploding Plastic Inevitable* failing, his fascination with the celebrities of the music world never ceased. As interest in his work was renewed, Warhol stepped further into the music world, first by meeting with David Bowie and inspiring the musician's Ziggy Stardust stage show, and later by designing the cover for the Rolling Stones's 1971 album *Sticky Fingers*, which featured the front of a pair of jeans with a working zipper. He also created the band's lapping-tongue logo, which remains a world-famous symbol even today.

In fact, he had every intention of returning to painting when the price was right. With one of his soup can paintings selling for $60,000 in May of 1970, at that time the most ever paid at auction for the work of a living American artist, it appeared the price was beginning to get into the desired ballpark.

The renewed interest in Warhol the painter continued in 1971, but now it was international. The Warhol retrospective had opened in Paris in late 1970. In early 1971, it opened in London. In West Germany, collectors and museums sought Warhol paintings, and *Flesh* was one of the country's top ten films of the year.

Warhol made a triumphant return to the New York art scene in April, when the Whitney Museum's version of the retrospective opened. The reviews were universally positive.

The Death of Julia Warhola

Julia Warhola's health went downhill after Warhol was shot. Julia was slipping into senility, failing to take her medication, and sometimes wandering away and getting lost. In February of 1971, she had a stroke and was hospitalized.

Even as an adult, Warhol remained close with his mother, Julia, who lived with him in New York City for a number of years. Julia was her son's biggest fan and most ardent supporter.

When she got out of the hospital, Paul Warhola and his wife Ann took her to Pittsburgh, but it was difficult for them. Julia would get up every morning and claim she was going back to New York. By the end of a month, she didn't know where she was.

Then she suffered a second stroke and lay in the hospital in a coma for several weeks. She recovered enough to leave the hospital, but, unable to care for her anymore, Paul and Ann put her in the Wightman Manor nursing home.

On November 22, 1972, Warhol's mother died in Pittsburgh. Warhol paid the funeral expenses, but he didn't attend. "Andy didn't want to see nobody dead," said his brother Paul. "He was deathly afraid."[3]

"I think he always felt guilty that he hadn't taken care of her until the end, but he couldn't have," said Jed Johnson.[4]

"No one every fully comprehended her reasons for following Andy to New York," wrote David Bourdon in his biography of Warhol. "Had she needed Andy as much as he needed her? Clearly, she had been a major source of her son's tenacity, shrewdness, resilience, and playful humor, and she had obviously enjoyed her reputation as 'Andy Warhol's Mother.'"[5]

In one of her last interviews before she left New York, Julia Warhola said, "I'm so glad I'm his mother. He's great. That I did that, you know, that's really a creation, don't you think it's a creation to produce Andy Warhol? I, Mrs. Warhol, I sometimes don't believe it that I could do that. But you see all the things he does, the good and the bad and the lousy and the shocking . . . and the fairies and the girls and the boys and the drugs. It's all here, it's all in him

Warhol parties at Studio 54 with friends like singer Debbie Harry (*third from right*) and author Truman Capote (*second from right*) to celebrate a new issue of *Interview* magazine.

and he pours it out and he gives everything, so that's why he's a great artist."[6]

Warhol's Big Interview

Warhol had been considering dropping his magazine *Interview*, which had gone through multiple editors and lost money instead of making it. But Fred Hughes suggested instead that they change the magazine's focus. Instead of an underground film magazine written by poets and artists, he said, they should make it "a magazine for people like us!"

They eventually settled on Bob Colacello as the editor, and he quickly set the magazine's tone. "We're not interested in journalism so much as taste setting," he said.[7]

Of course, Warhol and all his activities were frequently featured.

Warhol's portrait business was booming, headed toward being a $1 million-a-year operation. Anyone could have a Warhol portrait done for $25,000. In addition to doing portraits of people like Mick Jagger, he began cultivating world leaders as portrait subjects, controversially cozying up to the wives of dictators, including Farah Diba, the wife of the Shah of Iran, and Imelda Marcos, the wife of the ruler of the Philippines.

> **"An artist is somebody who produces things that people don't need to have."**
> **—Andy Warhol**

Warhol worked hard, several hours a day, seven days a week, then went to parties in the evenings. His social circle included people like the fashion designer Halston, author Truman Capote, Bianca Jagger, and actress Liza Minnelli.

Thanks to Colacello's connections to the wife of the Shah of Iran, Warhol realized a lifelong dream on May 15, 1975, when he was invited to the White House. The occasion was a state dinner with the Shah.

That September, Warhol's book *The Philosophy of Andy Warhol*, full of his observations on love, fame, beauty, and money, was published. His short version of his philosophy: "Everything is nothing." He also liked to say that the most exciting thing about making anything was "not doing it."[8]

According to Bob Colacello, Warhol's "not doing it" philosophy extended to the writing of his book. Colacello said he mostly wrote four chapters, Pat Hackett wrote nine, Brigid Berlin wrote one, and all three of them worked on the prologue. When he saw Warhol photographed for the cover of *New York* magazine, sitting at a typewriter, Colacello said, "It finally hit me then—I was part of a big lie and while it had lined my pockets, it robbed my ego of any hope of recognition."[9]

THE NATIONAL GALLERY

Warhol was not only a guest at the White House—he's a staple in Washington, DC. A combination of some of Warhol's most famous works, as well as some of his lesser-known paintings and sketches, are part of the National Gallery of Art. The Gallery has more than 200 works by the artist, and as of press time, fifteen were on view. His work has even been hung in the White House itself. In 2009, a Christmas ornament bearing a copy of one of his Mao paintings hung on one of the White House Christmas trees.

Warhol's Final Film

In 1976, Warhol filmed *Bad*. It was supposed to be low budget, but it ended up costing more than $1.2 million. Warhol refused to put any money into it himself. In order to save the project, Fred Hughes put in $200,000, his entire life savings. It was the only 1970s Warhol film not directed by Paul Morrissey; instead, that task fell to Jed Johnson. Pat Hackett provided the script.

Carroll Baker starred as a woman who ran an electrolysis business during the day and at night sent out an all-girl hit squad to commit crimes for her clients. The movie flopped. Warhol never made another film.

Instead, he showed a renewed focus on art. In 1977, Warhol's first major New York show since the *Silver Pillows* show back in 1966 opened in Leo Castelli's gallery. The paintings, some of the largest Warhol had done since the Mao portraits, featured the hammer and sickle—the symbols of Communism—but not arranged as they were on the flag of the Soviet Union.

Then, in 1977, as Warhol's life approached its final decade, something new arrived on the New York social scene: a club called Studio 54.

7

Taking It to the Street Artists

S tudio 54 was the creation of two men, Steve Rubell and Ian Schraeger, and it immediately became the place to be seen in New York—assuming you were rich, powerful, beautiful, or famous enough to get in. The club's central decorating feature was also a pretty good indication of what went on there. It was a neon sign in the shape of the Man in the Moon, which dropped from the ceiling and sniffed cocaine, represented by twinkling lights, up its nose.

Warhol was fascinated by Studio 54. It became almost a second office for him, a place where he found new people to work at the Factory, to paint, or to be interviewed for *Interview*. The magazine had become a great success partially because it was, in a way, Studio 54 in print—a place to be seen just for the sake of being seen.

According to Jed Johnson, the opening of Studio 54 coincided with a change in Warhol. "That was New York when it was at the height of its most decadent period . . . Andy was just wasting his time, and it was really upsetting . . . He just spent his time with the most ridiculous people."[1]

As had become his custom, Warhol tape-recorded everything and took a lot of photographs.

Celebrating the coming year on December 31, 1978, Warhol joined friends like Halston, Liza Minnelli, and Bianca Jagger at Studio 54 to say farewell to 1978 and welcome 1979.

Profitable Portraits

Portraits continued to be Warhol's most profitable line of business. He painted a series called *Athletes*, which featured Kareem Abdul Jabar, Muhammad Ali, Chris Evert, Dorothy Hamill, Jack Nicklaus, Pele, Tom Seaver, Willi Shoemaker, and O.J. Simpson. The sale of paintings and prints from the series eventually brought in $1 million.

Warhol attended events not just at Studio 54, but elsewhere, too—he once said he'd go to the opening of anything, even a toilet seat. Despite the nightly parties, he

WARHOL ROCKS!

Musically, the era was divided between punk and disco. Punks claimed Warhol for their own when he went to Europe for the opening of his *Hammer and Sickle Show* in Paris, but thanks to Studio 54, he was really more associated with disco. Nevertheless, he dipped his toe into the music world again by managing his own punk-rock musician, Walter Steding, who also worked as a painting assistant. He put out a Steding album on his own music label, Earhol, but it failed. Steding was eventually fired by Warhol—who rarely fired anyone—when he was several hours late for work.

turned out an enormous number of paintings during this period. He was churning out not only portraits, but also commissions for shows in several countries, and a great deal of his own work, too.

Warhol finally had another New York opening in January of 1979, when *Shadows*, a series of massive paintings based on photographs of shadows, opened at the Heiner Freidrich Gallery. They sold out before the show even opened.

Warhol Turns Fifty

That August, Warhol celebrated his fiftieth birthday at Studio 54. Halston hosted it. His presents included a pair of roller skates, a garbage pail full of $1 bills (which were

Like many of his passion projects, Warhol's book *Exposures* was a commercial failure.

dumped over his head), and 5,000 free Studio 54 drink tickets.

Grosset and Dunlap, a New York publishing house, announced shortly afterward the launch of Andy Warhol Books. The first book from the new imprint would be a collection of his photos of celebrities, called *Andy Warhol's Exposures*. It would be followed by a memoir of the 1960s called *POPism*, written with Pat Hackett.

On November 19, 1979, a huge collection of fifty-six of the portraits that had been his bread and butter throughout the decade opened at the Whitney Museum. Some of the subjects, such as Sylvester Stallone and Truman Capote, were at the star-studded reception.

Critical remarks about the show seemed to be aimed at Warhol as much as the art. "The faces are ugly and a shade stoned, if not actually repulsive and grotesque," wrote the *New York Times*, which called the work "shallow and boring" and commented on "the debased and brutalized feeling that characterizes every element of this style. That this . . . may be deliberate does not alter the offence."[1]

Which just showed, as critic Peter Schjeldahl wrote, that "Warhol has, once again, hit some kind of nerve."[2]

Over at Studio 54, meanwhile, the party was ending. In January, owners Steve Rubell and Ian Schrager were sentenced to three and a half years in prison and fined $20,000 each for tax evasion. One of the triggers for the bust by the Internal Revenue Service was a *New York* magazine cover in November that listed Studio 54's "Party Favors," including drugs for various celebrities and "$800 for Andy Warhol's Garbage Pail on his Birthday."[3]

Looking Backward

As seemed to be the case more often than not, various Warhol associates were having serious personal struggles. And Warhol was once again alienating the people around him, including Fred Hughes and Bob Colacello.

Jed Johnson moved out of Warhol's house in 1980, leaving Warhol depressed. He redoubled his efforts to cram the house full of stuff, going on regular shopping expeditions to flea markets.

Warhol also suddenly decided to take better care of himself. He gave up drinking, started eating health food, and worked out every day with a personal trainer.

The attempted assassination in 1968 still weighed on him. In a 1981 interview, he told a German reporter that "I'm afraid. I'm nervous . . . by chance I opened a letter in which it said, 'Live or die,' and yesterday the letter writer called me. We called the police but they can't do anything until you're killed."[4]

He cheered up, though, when he fell in love with a thirty-year-old man named Jon Gould, who moved in with him in 1983. Although Gould was never seen in public as Warhol's companion, according to Warhol's friends, the relationship bolstered Andy's spirits. "Jon was a light inside his life," said one.[5]

Other relationships, however, continued to fall apart, among them Andy's relationship with Bob Colacello, editor of *Interview*. Warhol seemed to feel Colacello was trying to take over. The final straw came when Colacello demanded a share of *Interview*. Warhol turned him down. Colacello left the Factory for good in February of 1983.

On the other hand, Warhol was cultivating relationships with the new generation of New York artists, who were

JEAN-MICHEL BASQUIAT

Born in 1960 in Brooklyn, Jean-Michel Basquiat had shown a talent for drawing at a young age, and gained notoriety as a graffiti artist before moving into fine art. Warhol met him in 1979, but despite Basquiat's talent, for a long time Warhol wouldn't meet with him or let him into the Factory, perhaps because of his reputation for being unpredictable—and a drug user. But Basquiat's talent was hard to ignore—Warhol knew it from the first time he'd met the young artist—and in June 1980, during Basquiat's first solo show, the world discovered his talent. Over the next few years, Basquiat would work with musicians and Warhol friends Blondie and David Bowie, and would show his work in the famous Gagosian Gallery in Los Angeles. Though he died in 1988, Basquiat remains one of the most famous and well-known artists in the world.

working in a suddenly booming art marketplace. Two groups in particular were attracted to him. One was the Neo-Expressionists, whose work featured strong brushstrokes, contrasting colors, and distorted subjects. Their paintings were typically large, sometimes featured found objects, and were created quickly.

The other group was made up of graffiti artists, of whom the best known was a young man named Jean-Michel Basquiat.

In 1983, Warhol's Swiss art dealer, Bruno Bischofberger, put up money for a series of three-way collaborations among Warhol, Jean-Michel Basquiat, and another artist, Francesco Clemente. The resulting works weren't received as enthusiastically as Bischofberger had hoped, but Warhol and Basquiat had hit it off, and Basquiat stayed at the Factory to work on more paintings with Warhol. In a unique collaborative process, they would pass the canvases back and forth, each adding new elements. "In the end they looked like a succession of brilliant defacements of each other's work," says Victor Bockris.[6] In one of them, *Brown Spots*, Basquiat portrayed Warhol as a banana. In another, Warhol portrayed Basquiat as Michelangelo's *David*—except David doesn't wear a jockstrap.

Other new young artists of the 1980s also seemed to have an affinity for Warhol, who in turn seemed to have an affinity for them. After all, he'd done the whole avant-garde thing long before they arrived on the scene; it made him a kind of aging role model.

Deteriorating Relationships

As often happened with Warhol, though, advances in his career were counterbalanced by problems in his personal

Jean-Michel Basquiat (*left*) helped introduce Warhol to a new generation of art lovers in the 1980s when the street artist paired with the Pop superstar for a series of collaborative works.

life. His boyfriend, Jon Gould, was diagnosed with AIDS, which had already claimed several of Warhol's more distant friends. Even though Warhol hated hospitals, when Gould spent several weeks in New York Hospital in 1985, Warhol visited him every day, sometimes staying for hours.

After he got out of the hospital, Gould left Warhol's house and moved to Los Angeles. Warhol felt betrayed and soon refused to talk about him.

Gould died in September 1986.

Meanwhile, Warhol's relationship with Basquiat was also deteriorating. Basquiat wasn't handling his success well, wasting money on silly extravagances. After he read something in the *New York Times* suggesting he was too influenced by Warhol, he stopped talking to Warhol. When their joint show opened in September of 1985, neither man spoke to the other.

Still, Warhol kept drawing in new people—or going to them. He loved hanging out with rock stars like Madonna, Grace Jones, and Sting. He attended the wedding of Maria Shriver and Arnold Schwarzenegger. He continued to work hard on commissions from all over the world. But to his associates, despite his frantic pace, he seemed lonely and depressed.

Final Works

In the summer of 1986, Warhol painted a final series of self-portraits, based on a photograph of him in which his wig was sticking up at wild angles. John Caldwell bought one for the Carnegie Museum in Philadelphia, where, as a child, Warhol had taken art lessons. Of the painting, Caldwell wrote, "He looks simultaneously ravaged and

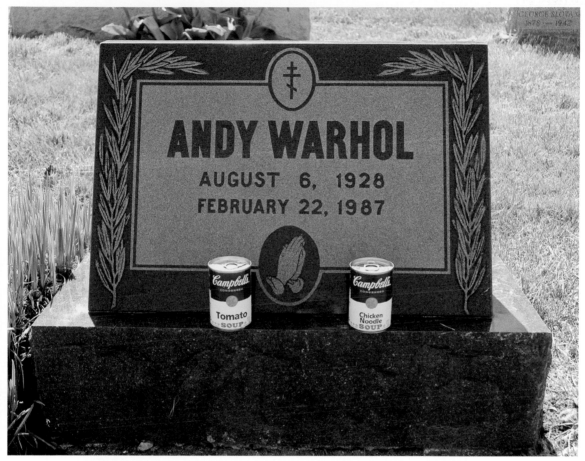

Fans who visit Warhol's grave often leave behind mementos to the artist, including cans of Campbell's soup — in honor of his famous early paintings.

demonic, blank and full of too many years and too much experience."[7]

The portraits were well received when they were shown in London in July. Warhol seemed a bit happier when he returned. Various other enterprises continued to go well. Warhol had found a new outlet for his film and television aspirations: directing music videos for bands like the Cars and making cameos in some of them. *Interview* continued to prosper.

The Death of Andy Warhol

The pain from his stomach was continuing to plague him. It was a sign of how much it was bothering him when he decided to stay home instead of going out on the night of February 13, 1987, because Warhol always went out.

On February 18, he visited his doctor, who diagnosed an acutely infected gallbladder that needed to be removed right away. Warhol wanted to put it off for a few more days, but a second ultrasound showed the gallbladder to be severely inflamed and filled with fluid.

The plan was for Andy to have the operation on Saturday and be out on Sunday. No one but his closest aides knew. He checked in to New York Hospital under an assumed name, Bob Robert. The surgery was performed between 8:45 a.m. and 12:10 p.m. on Saturday, February 21, and there were no complications.

At 5:45 a.m. the next morning, the nurse noticed that the sleeping Warhol had turned blue and his pulse had weakened. A cardiac arrest team was unable revive him and he was pronounced dead at 6:31 a.m., apparently from a heart attack. The New York State Department of Health later concluded that "the active medical staff of the hospital did not assure the maintenance of the proper quality of all medication and treatment provided to patient." A wrongful-death suit was brought against the hospital by Warhol's estate, and was settled out of court for $3 million.[8]

CNN broke the news at noon on Sunday. The next day it was on the front pages of newspapers around the world. Warhol's associates, most of whom hadn't even known he was ill, were shocked.

On February 26, Warhol was laid to rest. A simple marble slab, carved with Warhol's name and the dates of his birth and death, marked his grave.

A priest said a prayer and sprinkled holy water on the casket, but the last things to go into the grave before it was filled in was a copy of *Interview* and a bottle of Estée Lauder perfume.[9]

CONCLUSION

More than three decades have passed since Andy Warhol's death, and he continues to be a polarizing figure. People either love him or hate him, but very few are indifferent to him.

One thing that seems obvious is that he's not going away. Major exhibitions of his work continue to be mounted on a regular basis, not only because curators and critics see the work as important, but also because a Warhol show is sure to draw a crowd.

His immediate legacy, of course, was his enormous estate, estimated conservatively to be worth $200 million at the time of his death, but possibly worth as much as $500 million. In his will, Warhol stipulated that the bulk of his wealth should go to create a foundation dedicated to the "advancement of the visual arts."

In accordance with his wishes, the Warhol Foundation was created. Between 1990 and 2001, the Foundation converted the art bequeathed to it by Warhol into more than $131 million in cash and investments, while distributing more than $41 million in grants to help advance the visual arts.

Warhol's fortune, through the Warhol Foundation, has also helped establish Creative Capital, a foundation to support individual artists. In its first five years, Creative Capital helped more than 150 artists with cash grants and career development advice. The Warhol Foundation recently gave Creative Capital an additional ten-year, $10 million gift to continue its work.

Another Foundation project, the Warhol Initiative, provided substantial support to thirty-one small- to

In the more than three decades since Warhol passed away, his celebrity has never diminished. His work remains on display around the world, and his influence on popular culture is undeniable.

mid-sized artist-based organizations, helping them achieve greater financial security so they could continue their services to artists and art audiences.

In 1994, the Foundation started the Andy Warhol Museum in the artist's hometown of Pittsburgh, stocking it with more than 3,900 works of art—not just paintings, but also drawings, photographs, prints, film and video, sculpture, and archival material from the Warhol estate.

While he was alive, Warhol made a concerted effort to market not only his art, but also his name. He appeared in ads and loaned his name to various projects. The Foundation is following in his footsteps. There's a whole line of Andy Warhol products that fans can purchase, including clothing, housewares, and stationery, among other commercial items.

The real legacy of Warhol isn't his fame or fortune, but his art. And there's a lot of it—it's estimated he created some 32,000 paintings and prints during his lifetime.[1] Shortly after his death, critics began to look at his life's work with fresh eyes.

Although "hitching his wagon" to stars like Marilyn Monroe and Elvis Presley and using pop culture

In 2003, the Andy Warhol Museum, located in Pittsburgh, Pennsylvania, celebrated what would have been the artist's seventy-fifth birthday.

A New York City dog shows up to a 2016 canine Halloween parade dressed as Warhol, proving that the artist may be gone, but he will never be forgotten.

references like Campbell's Soup cans in his work, Warhol made himself into a kind of "mythic figure and cultural emblem of his times," says biographer David Bourdon. "Warhol was also a gifted artist . . . Bucking the prevailing trend of painterly abstraction, he injected new freshness and vitality in some of the most traditional categories of painting—portraits, still lifes, and genre." His willingness to use anything and everything from the mass media in his work has expanded the range of subject matter available to painters.

Warhol museum director Thomas Sokolowski points out that YouTube is the embodiment of Warhol's most famous quote: "In the future everybody will be world-famous for fifteen minutes," (which, he notes, Warhol actually lifted from a "more boring text" by media critic Marshall McLuhan). On YouTube, "you can have a four-year-old sneaking some Peppermint schnapps at her birthday and suddenly everyone knows about it. If that's not fifteen minutes of fame it's fifteen seconds of fame." Warhol saw that coming long before anyone else did, Sokolowski says—and realized the pitfalls. "He understood that with this new fame, this new engagement with the world, we are opening up a Pandora's box."[2]

There is a tendency—one Warhol himself rather encouraged, with his flippant remarks about his own art—to think of him as nothing more than a brand name, like the Coke bottles or Campbell's Soup cans he painted.

But even as his Foundation markets his name and images all over the world, more than thirty years after his death, it's becoming more and more obvious that he was far more than a mere brand. Love him or loathe him, he was, without a doubt, a true American rebel.

CHRONOLOGY

On August 6, Andrew Warhola is born in Pittsburgh to Julia and Ondrej Warhola.

Andy starts attending free Saturday art classes at the Carnegie Museum.

His father, Ondrej Warhola, dies after a lengthy illness.

Andy Warhola enrolls in the Department of Painting and Design at the Carnegie Institute of Technology (presently Carnegie Mellon University).

Warhola experiments with the blotted-line drawing technique that he will use to great effect as a commercial artist; he has two paintings in the annual exhibition of the Associated Artists of Pittsburgh.

Warhola moves to New York City and begins working as a commercial artist, using the name Andy Warhol.

Warhol's first solo exhibition, *Fifteen Drawings Based on the Writings of Truman Capote*, opens at the Hugo Gallery.

Warhol begins making his own illustrated books, which he gives to clients and associates and sells in shops.

Warhol exhibits work in both group and solo shows at the Loft Gallery in New York City.

Warhol is chosen by the shoe company I. Miller to illustrate its weekly newspaper advertisements.

1957   Andy Warhol Enterprises is legally incorporated.

1960–1961   Warhol paints his first works based on comics and advertisements.

1962   Warhol begins using photo-silkscreen technique.

1963–1964   Warhol shoots a number of films, including *Eat*, *Empire*, and *Harlot* (his first film with live sound).

1965   Warhol announces in Paris he is retiring from painting in order to devote himself to film.

1966–1967   Warhol produces the first album by the Velvet Underground and Nico and designs the cover with a peelable banana.

1968   On June 3, Valerie Solanas shoots Warhol.

1969   The first issue of *Interview* magazine is published.

1971   Warhol designs the album cover of the Rolling Stones' *Sticky Fingers*; cover is nominated for a Grammy Award.

1972   Julia Warhol dies in Pittsburgh.

1974   Warhol begins assembling *Time Capsules*.

1979   *Andy Warhol's Exposures*, with photographs by Warhol, is published.

1983   Warhol, Jean-Michel Basquiat, and Francesco Clemente begin collaborating on paintings; Warhol and Basquiat become close friends and continue working together.

1987   After several days of acute pain, Warhol enters New York Hospital for gallbladder surgery; dies in hospital of a heart attack on February 22.

CHAPTER NOTES

Introduction

1. Bockris, Victor, *Warhol*. (New York, NY: Da Capo Press, 1997). p. 149.

2. "The Slice-of Cake School." *Time* Magazine, Friday, May 11, 1962, http://www.time.com/time/magazine/article/0,9171,939397,00.html (November 5, 2008).

3. Kaplan, Justin, ed. *Bartlett's Familiar Quotations*, 16th Ed. (New York, NY: Little, Brown & Co., 1992), p. 758.

4. Vogel, Carol. "Modern Acquires 2 Icons Of Pop Art." The New York Times, October 10, 1996.

Chapter 1: A Colorful Childhood

1. Bockris, p. 24.

2. "Julia Warhola - Andy Warhol's Mother." The Andy Warhol Family Album, http://www.warhola.com/andysmother.html (November 5, 2008).

3. Bockris, p. 33.

4. Warhol, Andy and Pat Hackett, *POPism: The Warhol Sixties* (New York, NY: Harcourt Brace Jovanovich, 1980).

5. "Rheumatic Fever." Mayo Clinic.com, http://www.mayoclinic.com/health/rheumatic-fever/DS00250 (November 6, 2008).

Chapter 2: Welcome to New York

1. Guiles, Fred Lawrence *Loner at the Ball: The Life of Andy Warhol*, (New York, NY: Bantam Press, 1989), p. 18.

2. Bockris, Victor, *Warhol*, (New York, NY: Da Capo Press, 1997), pp 50-51.

3. Ibid, p. 52.

4. Bockris, p. 65.

5. Ibid, p. 67.

6. Johnson, Seth. "From the Bauhaus to the 21st Century," http://web.utk.edu/~art/faculty/kennedy/bauhaus/index.html (November 6, 2008).

7. "Blotted Line Drawing," The Warhol: Resources and Lessons, http://edu.warhol.org/aract_blot.html (November 6, 2008).

8. Bockris, p. 77.

9. Bockris, p. 81.

10. Ibid, p. 89.

11. Bourdon, David, *Warhol*, (New York, NY: Harry N. Abrams, Inc., 1989), p. 32.

12. Coplans, John, et al., *Andy Warhol*, (New York, NY: Little, Brown & Co., 1970).

13. Bockris, p. 115.

14. Smith, Patrick S, *Andy Warhol's Art and Films*, (Ann Arbor, MI: UMI Research Press, 1986), p. 372.

15. Bockris, p. 125.

16. Iacono, Amanda Lo, "'My highlight of 2015'—Warhol's Golden Shoe," Christie's, http://www.christies.com/features/My-highlight-of-2015-ANdy-Warhol-Golden-Shoe-6910-1.aspx (March 14, 2017).

17. "Robert Rauschenberg - About the Artist." American Masters, http://www.pbs.org/wnet/americanmasters/episodes/robert-rauschenberg/about-the-artist/49 (June 5, 2009).

18. "Jasper Johns - About the Painter." American Masters, http://www.pbs.org/wnet/americanmasters/episodes/jasper-johns/about-the-painter/54/ (June 5, 2009).

19. Ibid.

20. Kornbluth, Jesse, *Pre-Pop Warhol*, (New York, NY: Panache Press, 1988), pp. 17-18.

21. Bockris, p. 131.

22. Gardner, Helen *Art Through the Ages* (Sixth Edition), (New York, NY: Harcourt Brace Javanovich, 1975.) pp. 782-784.

23. Bockris, p. 136.

24. Ibid, p. 140.

25. Ibid, p. 142.

26. Ibid, p. 143.

27. Comenas, Gary, "The Origin of Andy Warhol's Soup Cans," Warholstars, http://www.warholstars.org/art/Warhol/soup.html (November 8, 2008).

Chapter 3: Factory Setting

1. "Andy Warhol's Methods and Techniques," The Andy Warhol Museum, http://www.warhol.org/education/pdfs/methods_and_techs.pdf (November 8, 2008).

2. Smith, Patrick S, *Andy Warhol's Art and Films*, (Ann Arbor, MI: UMI Research Press, 1981) pp. 504-505.

3. Fried, Michael, "New York Letter," *Art International*, December 20, 1962.

4. Bockris, Victor, *Warhol*, (New York, NY: Da Capo Press, 1997), p. 156.

5. Ibid, p. 157.

6. "Pop Art: Cult of the Commonplace," *TIME* Magazine, May 3, 1963, http://www.time.com/time/magazine/article/0,9171,828186-1,00.html (June 5, 2009).

7. Vogel, Carol, "Grisly Warhol Painting Fetches $104.5 Million, Auction High for Artist," *New York Times*, November 13, 2013.

8. Greenhalgh, Paul, *Quotations and sources on design and the decorative arts*, (New York, NY: Manchester University Press, 1993). p. 53.

9. Bockris, p. 187

10. Sooke, Alastair, "Jackie Kennedy: Andy Warhol's pop saint," BBC.com, http://www.bbc.com/culture/

story/20140418-jackie-warhols-pop-saint (March 14, 2017).

11. Warhol, Andy and Pat Hackett, *POPism: The Warhol Sixties* (New York, NY: Harcourt Brace Jovanovich, 1980), p. 73.

12. Bockris, p. 192.

13. Warhol & Hackett, pp. 71-72

14. Bockris, p. 199.

15. Bourdon, David, "Andy Warhol and the American Dream," *Andy Warhol: 1928-1987*, (Munich, Germany: Prestel-Verlag, 1993). p. 10.

16. Webster, Norman, "What is art? Ask Canadian Customs inspectors," *Montreal Gazette*, November 9, 2008.

17. Bockris, p. 224.

Chapter 4: Fifteen Minutes of Film Fame

1. Ramanathan, Lavanya, "'Sleep': Warhol's 5-Hour Fever Dream," *Washington Post,* April 3, 2008, p. C13.

2. Giorno, John. "My 15 Minutes," *Guardian*, February 14, 2002.

3. Warhol, Andy and Pat Hackett, *POPism: The Warhol Sixties* (New York, NY: Harcourt Brace Jovanovich, 1980), p. 32.

4. Bockris, p. 191.

5. Honnef, Klaus, *Andy Warhol 1928-1987: Commerce into Art*, (Koln, Germany: Benedikt Taschen Verlag, 1993), pp. 79-80.

6. Bockris, p. 207.

7. Indiana, Gary, "Mary Woronov," *Interview*, June-July, 2008.

8. Stein, Jean with George Plimpton. *Edie: An American Biography* (New York, NY: Alfred A. Knopf, 1982), p. 234.

9. Crimp, Douglas, "Coming Together to Stay Apart," Warholstars, http://www.warholstars.org/tavel_crimp.html (June 5, 2009).

10. Bockris, Warhol, p. 257

11. Dufresne, Isabelle Collin (Ultra Violet), *Famous for 15 Minutes: My Years with Andy Warhol*, (New York, NY: Harcourt Brace Jovanovich, 1988), p. 169.

Chapter 5: Attacked by SCUM

1. Colacello, Bob, *Holy Terror: Andy Warhol Close Up*, (New York, NY: Harper Collins, 1990), p. 32.

2. Ibid, p. 278.

3. Ibid, p. 279.

4. Hughes, Robert, "The Rise of Andy Warhol," *New York Review of Books*, vol. 29, no. 2, 1982.

5. Bockris, p. 283.

6. Warhol, Andy and Pat Hackett, *POPism: The Warhol Sixties* (New York, NY: Harcourt Brace Jovanovich, 1980), p. 265.

7. Marmorstein, Robert, "SCUM Goddess: A Winter Memory of Valerie Solanis," *Village Voice*, June 13, 1968, p. 9-10, 20

8. Bourdon, David, *Warhol*, (New York, NY: Harry N. Abrams, Inc., 1989), p. 284.

9. Bockris, p. 302.

10. Ibid, p. 303.

11. Bourdon, p. 286,

12. "Felled by Scum," *TIME* Magazine, Friday, June 14, 1968, http://www.time.com/time/0,8816,900118,00.html (November 10, 2008).

13. Ibid, p. 311.

Chapter 6: Retirement, Cut Short

1. Bockris, Victor, *Warhol* (New York, NY: Da Capo Press, 1997), p. 327.

2. Ibid, p. 335.

3. Bockris, p. 362.

4. Ibid, p. 363.

5. Ibid., p. 243.

6. Andy Warhol, *Transcript of David Bailey's ATV Documentary* (London, UK: Bailey Litchfield/Mathews Miller Dunbar Ltd., 1972).

7. Bockris, p. 363.

8. Ibid, p. 390

9. Colacello, p. 308.

Chapter 7: Taking It to the Street Artists

1. Kramer, Hilton, "Art: Whitney shows Warhol Works," *New York Times*, November 23, 1979.

2. Schjeldahl, Peter, "Warhol and Class Content," Art in America, May, 1980.

3. Colacello, Bob, *Holy Terror: Andy Warhol Close Up* (New York, NY: Harper Collins, 1990), p. 423.

4. Windmuller, Eva, "A Conversation with Andy Warhol," Stern, October 8, 1981.

5. Bockris, p. 445.

6. Bockris, p 460.

7. Caldwell, John, Carnegie Mellon Magazine, 1986.

8. Alexander, Paul, *Death and Disaster: The Rise of the Warhol Empire and the Race for Andy's Millions*, (New York, NY: Villard Books, 1994), p. 96.

9. Bockris, p. 494.

Conclusion

1. Ibid.

2. Sokolowski.

GLOSSARY

agent An artist's business representative, who negotiates contracts and collects money.

amphetamine A drug that stimulates the central nervous system.

art critic A person who describes, analyzes, and evaluates artworks, usually for a newspaper, magazine, or other publication.

avant-garde French for "vanguard"; artists who are innovative or experimental, and whose work is ahead of its time.

barbiturate A drug that depresses the central nervous system, sometimes used to promote sleep.

cocaine An addictive drug that produces a feeling of euphoria.

collage A picture or design created by adhering items such as newspaper clippings, photographs, or cloth to a flat surface.

commercial art The creation of images or objects for commercial and advertising purposes.

counterculture A culture with values that run counter to those of established society.

curator In art, a person who is responsible for collecting, caring for, researching, showing, and writing about an exhibition.

disco A form of dance music, popular in the 1970s that features hypnotic rhythm, repetitive lyrics, and electronically produced sounds.

entourage A group of attendants and associates.

fine art Art created for its own sake, as opposed to being created for commercial purposes.

gallery A place for displaying and selling art.

one-man show An exhibition of art that has all been created by the same person.

portfolio A collection of pieces that an artist uses to show prospective clients the kind of work he or she is capable of.

punk rock Rock music that features extreme and often deliberately offensive expressions of social discontent.

realism Art that realistically depicts people, places, or things.

retrospective An exhibit that covers the body of work of a particular artist or group of artists.

underground film A film set apart by its style, genre, or financing that is typically not shown in mainstream movie theaters.

FURTHER READING

Books

Anderson, Kirsten. *Who Was Andy Warhol?* New York, NY: Grosset & Dunlap, 2014.

Fraser-Cavassoni, Natasha. *After Andy: Adventures in Warhol Land*. New York, NY: Bluerider Press, 2017.

Hackett, Pat. *The Andy Warhol Diaries*. New York, NY: Warner Books, 2014.

Websites

The Andy Warhol Museum

www.warhol.org

A museum founded by the Andy Warhol Foundation and dedicated to Warhol's life and art, it is the most comprehensive collection of biographical information about and artwork by Warhol.

Interview Magazine

www.interviewmagazine.com

The magazine founded by Andy Warhol, Interview *remains a top lifestyle and art magazine that continues to inform the tastes of the rich and famous.*

Films

Burns, Ric. *Andy Warhol: A Documentary Film*. PBS, 2006.

Workman, Chuck. *The Life & Times of Andy Warhol—Superstar*. Shout Factory, 2003.

INDEX